Antony and Cleopatra

William Shakespeare

Edited, fully annotated, and introduced by Burton Raffel

With an essay by Harold Bloom

THE ANNOTATED SHAKESPEARE

Yale University Press • New Haven and London

Designed by Rebecca Gibb.
Set in Bembo type by The Composing Room of Michigan, Inc.
Printed in the United States of America by R. R. Donnelley & Sons.

Library of Congress Cataloging-in-Publication Data
Shakespeare, William, 1564–1616.
Antony and Cleopatra / William Shakespeare ; edited, fully annotated,
and introduced by Burton Raffel;
with an essay by Harold Bloom.
p.   cm. — (The annotated Shakespeare)
Includes bibliographical references.
ISBN 978-0-300-12473-6 (pbk.)
1. Antonius, Marcus, 83?–30 B.C.—Drama.   2. Cleopatra, Queen of Egypt,
d. 30 B.C.—Drama.   3. Rome—History—Civil War, 43–31 B.C.—Drama.
4. Egypt—History—332–30 B.C.—Drama.   5. Romans—Egypt—Drama.
6. Queens—Egypt—Drama.   I. Raffel, Burton.   II. Bloom, Harold.
III. Title.
PR2802.A2R34 2007
822.3'3—dc22
2007021005

A catalogue record for this book is available from the British Library.

10 9 8 7 6 5 4 3 2 1

To Katherine Staples

CONTENTS

ABOUT THIS BOOK

*A*ntony and Cleopatra is not quite so densely strewn with historically produced linguistic prickles as are most of Shakespeare's plays. But it can be difficult going. Here is a brief scene between an angry Antony and a patient Cleopatra:

Cleopatra Have you done yet?
Antony   Alack, our terrene moon
   Is now eclipsed, and it portends alone
   The fall of Antony.
Cleopatra   I must stay his time.
Antony   To flatter Caesar, would you mingle eyes
   With one that ties his points?
Cleopatra   Not know me yet?
Antony   Cold-hearted toward me?

This was perfectly understandable, we must assume, to the mostly very average persons who paid to watch Elizabethan plays. But who today can make full or comfortable sense of it? In this very fully annotated edition, I therefore present this passage, not in the bare form quoted above, but thoroughly supported by bottom-of-the-page notes:

Cleopatra Have you done yet?
Antony   Alack, our terrene moon[1]
   Is now eclipsed, and it portends alone[2]
   The fall of Antony.
Cleopatra   I must stay his time.[3]
Antony To flatter Caesar, would you mingle eyes[4]
   With one that ties his points?[5]
Cleopatra   Not know[6] me yet?
Antony Cold-hearted toward me?

Without full explanation of words that have over the years shifted in meaning, and usages that have been altered, neither the modern reader nor the modern listener is likely to be equipped for anything like full comprehension.

I believe annotations of this sort create the necessary bridges, from Shakespeare's four-centuries-old English across to ours. Some readers, to be sure, will be able to comprehend unusual, historically different meanings without any glosses. Those not familiar with the modern meaning of particular words will easily find clear, simple definitions in any modern dictionary. But most readers are not likely to understand Shakespeare's intended meaning, absent such glosses as I here offer.

There are no serious textual problems, since the only Renaissance text of the play is the 1623 *Folio,* which I have here followed.

---

1 terrene moon = earthly ("human") moon goddess, Cleopatra★
2 portends alone = only predicts
3 stay his time = wait/be still/patient until he is ready
4 mingle eyes = associate, be friendly with
5 his points = Caesar's laces (i.e., a servant)
6 recognize

My annotation practices have followed the same principles used in *The Annotated Milton*, published in 1999, and in my annotated editions of *Hamlet*, published (as the initial volume in this series) in 2003, *Romeo and Juliet* (published in 2004), and subsequent volumes in this series. Classroom experience has validated these editions. Classes of mixed upper-level undergraduates and graduate students have more quickly and thoroughly transcended language barriers than ever before. This allows the teacher, or a general reader without a teacher, to move more promptly and confidently to the nonlinguistic matters that have made Shakespeare and Milton great and important poets.

It is the inevitable forces of linguistic change, operant in all living tongues, which have inevitably created such wide degrees of obstacles to ready comprehension—not only sharply different meanings, but subtle, partial shifts in meaning that allow us to think we understand when, alas, we do not. Speakers of related languages like Dutch and German also experience this shifting of the linguistic ground. Like early Modern English (ca. 1600) and the Modern English now current, those languages are too close for those who know only one language, and not the other, to be readily able always to recognize what they correctly understand and what they do not. When, for example, a speaker of Dutch says, "Men kofer is kapot," a speaker of German will know that something belonging to the Dutchman is broken ("kapot" = "kaputt" in German, and "men" = "mein"). But without more linguistic awareness than the average person is apt to have, the German speaker will not identify "kofer" ("trunk" in Dutch) with "Körper"—a modern German word meaning "physique, build, body." The closest word to "kofer" in modern German, indeed, is "Scrankkoffer," which is too large a leap for ready comprehension. Speakers of different Romance languages (French, Spanish, Italian), and all other related but not identical tongues, all experience these difficulties, as well as the difficulty of understanding a text written in their own language five, or six, or seven hundred years earlier. Shakespeare's English is not yet so old that it requires, like many historical texts in French and German, or like Old English texts—for example, *Beowulf*—a modern translation. Much poetry evaporates in translation: language is immensely particular. The sheer *sound* of Dante in thirteenth-century Italian is profoundly worth preserving. So too is the sound of Shakespeare.

I have annotated prosody (metrics) only when it seemed truly necessary or particularly helpful. Readers should have no problem with the silent "e" in past participles (loved, returned, missed). Except in the few instances where modern usage syllabifies the "e," whenever an "e" in Shakespeare is *not* silent, it is marked "è." The notation used for prosody, which is also used in the explanation of Elizabethan pronunciation, follows the extremely simple form of my *From Stress to Stress: An Autobiography of English Prosody* (see "Further Reading," near the end of this book). Syllables with metrical stress are capitalized; all other syllables are in lowercase letters. I have managed to employ normalized Elizabethan spellings, in most indications of pronunciation, but I have sometimes been obliged to deviate, in the higher interest of being understood.

I have annotated, as well, a limited number of such other matters, sometimes of interpretation, sometimes of general or historical relevance, as have seemed to me seriously worthy of inclusion. These annotations have been most carefully restricted: this is not intended to be a book of literary commentary. It is for that reason that the glossing of metaphors has been severely restricted.

There is almost literally no end to discussion and/or analysis of metaphor, especially in Shakespeare. To yield to temptation might well be to double or triple the size of this book—and would also change it from a historically oriented language guide to a work of an unsteadily mixed nature. In the process, I believe, neither language nor literature would be well or clearly served.

Where it seemed useful, and not obstructive of important textual matters, I have modernized spelling, including capitalization. Spelling is not on the whole a basic issue, but punctuation and lineation must be given high respect. The Folio (which is the sole source of our text) uses few exclamation marks or semicolons, which is to be sure a matter of the conventions of a very different era. Still, our modern preferences cannot be lightly substituted for what is, after a fashion, the closest thing to a Shakespeare manuscript we are likely ever to have. We do not know whether these particular seventeenth-century printers, like most of that time, were responsible for question marks, commas, periods, and, especially, all-purpose colons, or whether these particular printers tried to follow their handwritten sources. Nor do we know if those sources, or what part thereof, might have been in Shakespeare's own hand. But in spite of these equivocations and uncertainties, it remains true that, to a very considerable extent, punctuation tends to result from just how the mind responsible for that punctuating *hears* the text. And twenty-first-century minds have no business, in such matters, overruling seventeenth-century ones. Whoever the compositors were, they were more or less Shakespeare's contemporaries, and we are not.

Accordingly, when the original printed text uses a comma, we are being signaled that *they* (whoever "they" were) heard the text, not coming to a syntactic stop, but continuing to some later stopping point. To replace commas with editorial periods is thus risky and on the whole an undesirable practice. (The dramatic action of a tragedy, to be sure, may require us, for twenty-first-century readers, to highlight what four-hundred-year-old punctuation standards may not make clear—and may even, at times, misrepresent.)

When the printed text has a colon, what we are being signaled is that *they* heard a syntactic stop—though not necessarily or even usually the particular kind of syntactic stop we associate, today, with the colon. It is therefore inappropriate to substitute editorial commas for original colons. It is also inappropriate to employ editorial colons when *their* syntactic usage of colons does not match ours. In general, the closest thing to *their* syntactic sense of the colon is our (and their) period.

The printed interrogation (question) marks, too, merit extremely respectful handling. In particular, editorial exclamation marks should very rarely be substituted for interrogation marks.

It follows from these considerations that the movement and sometimes the meaning of what we must take to be Shakespeare's *play* will at times be different, depending on whose punctuation we follow, *theirs* or our own. I have tried, here, to use the printed seventeenth-century text as a guide to both *hearing* and *understanding* what Shakespeare wrote.

Since the original printed texts (there not being, as there never are for Shakespeare, any surviving manuscripts) are frequently careless as well as self-contradictory, I have been relatively free with the wording of stage directions—and in some cases have added brief directions, to indicate who is speaking to whom. I have made no emendations; I have necessarily been obliged to make choices. Textual decisions have been annotated when the differences between or among the original printed texts seem either marked or of unusual interest.

In the interests of compactness and brevity, I have employed in my annotations (as consistently as I am able) a number of stylistic and typographical devices:

- The annotation of a single word does not repeat that word

- The annotation of more than one word repeats the words being annotated, which are followed by an equals sign and then by the annotation; the footnote number in the text is placed after the last of the words being annotated

- In annotations of a single word, alternative meanings are usually separated by commas; if there are distinctly different ranges of meaning, the annotations are separated by arabic numerals inside parentheses—(1), (2), and so on; in more complexly worded annotations, alternative meanings expressed by a single word are linked by a forward slash, or solidus: /

- Explanations of textual meaning are not in parentheses; comments about textual meaning are

- Except for proper nouns, the word at the beginning of all annotations is in lower case

- Uncertainties are followed by a question mark, set in parentheses: (?)

- When particularly relevant, "translations" into twenty-first-century English have been added, in parentheses

- Annotations of repeated words are *not* repeated. Explanations of the *first* instance of such common words are followed by the sign ★. Readers may easily track down the first annotation, using the brief Finding List at the back of the book. Words with entirely separate meanings are annotated *only* for meanings no longer current in Modern English.

The most important typographical device here employed is the sign ★ *placed after the first (and only) annotation of words and phrases occurring more than once. There is an alphabetically arranged listing of such words and phrases in the Finding List at the back of the book. The Finding List contains no annotations but simply gives the words or phrases themselves and the numbers of the relevant act, the scene within that act, and the footnote number within that scene for the word's first occurrence.*

INTRODUCTION

The two plays immediately preceding *Antony and Cleopatra*, in the now reasonably well established canon of Shakespeare's plays, are two of the grandest dramas in the world's stage history, *Macbeth* and *King Lear*. Like them, *Antony and Cleopatra* (dating from 1606 to 1607) is a tragedy. Unlike them, it presents a panoramically broad portrait that includes an unusually large number of characters, figures ranging from very great to very small indeed.

A cast's size, of course, does not in and of itself determine dramatic structure or even narrative pace. In *Antony and Cleopatra*, Shakespeare has deployed a large cast to create continuous high activity, employing a brilliantly managed, virtuosic structure. Critics have rightly insisted on these basic matters. "The world of *Antony and Cleopatra* is so immense that time yawns in it"; "The vastness of the [play's] world exceeds geography and reaches out to include the sky, the sun, the moon, that stars, and the cosmos, the realms of fire and air"; "[It] is in some respects the most complex, sustained, and magnificent piece of musical orchestration to be found anywhere in Shakespeare."[1] Of all Shakespeare's plays, only *Hamlet* and *King Lear* run as long as *Antony and Cleopatra*. These are both well-paced plays with large casts, but *Hamlet* contains only twenty scenes, and *King Lear* twenty-six, whereas *Antony and Cleopatra* has forty-two. What this means, both in the theater and in private, silent reading, is that both the setting and the characters change more than twice as rapidly in *Antony and Cleopatra* as they do in *Hamlet,* and something less than twice as rapidly as they do in *King Lear.* This is almost a cinematic level of activity—a kind of constant ping-pong switching of audience- and reader-attention. The on-stage result is a beautifully focused and steadily accelerating dramatic tension, the progressive stages of which are carefully laid out for us, point by point. ("This universe is too large to be rendered in anything but fragments. . . . It can be handled only by a process of constantly reassembling its many small parts—moving them about in an always flexible mosaic.")[2]

Perhaps the best approach to a necessarily brief analysis of how *Antony and Cleopatra* evolves is to examine aspects of some of its constantly interacting themes. In a sense, the play is almost equally a historical drama, a love story, and a tragedy, a tripartite main thrust that, in turn, generates an unusually wide variety of sub-themes—how power is gained, and lost, and the effects of both such gain and such loss on moral and characterological values; the difficult balance between romantic love and power, and the very different love impetuses of men and of women; and, finally, how our human limitations inevitably close in around us. ("*Antony and Cleopatra*—unlike *Julius Caesar,* to which it is a sequel—is only partly a political play; perhaps not a political play even primarily, but a play of passion.")[3]

Antony and Cleopatra *as Historical Drama*

Shakespeare's audience, and Shakespeare himself, was plainly much preoccupied with historical stories in general. The deep interest in matters Roman, however, was part of an abiding, far-reaching Renaissance concern—both in England and all across Europe—for what was still regarded as the mother and model of great states and lasting civilizations. Then, and for another more than three hundred years, Austro-Hungary claimed to be an incarnation of the Holy Roman Empire. Just as Latin was without question the dominant language of intellectual discourse, and was also the basic subject of instruction in all but the most elementary of schools, so too Roman (and to a lesser extent Greek) mythology was, quite simply, "mythology." The names and something of the stories of Roman gods, and famous Roman men (and a few Roman women), were known to virtually everyone, whether or not literate or possessing any knowledge of Latin. "As for [Renaissance] theory and practice of historical writing," Douglas Bush has dryly observed, "it was the ancients who taught that."[4] George Puttenham's *The Arte of English Poesie* (1589) subtitles its second chapter even more revealingly: "That there may be an art of our English poesie, aswell [sic] as there is of the Latine and Greeke."[5]

Seven characters in *Julius Caesar* have died by the time the play ends. Six other conspirators are as good as dead. The two characters who triumph, in that play, Octavius and Mark Antony, fight yet another deadly war in *Antony and Cleopatra,* this time against each other, a war that Antony will not survive. In both plays, all those who die have plainly chosen (or will choose) their own fatal path. Many have been warned, and have multiple opportunities to reconsider; none do. If we label these determinedly death-oriented stances "stoic," we will be in good part correct, for Stoicism is indeed a set of beliefs central to the Roman way of life. Neither pain nor pleasure mattered a great deal, according to this strongly fatalistic viewpoint. And death, when at its own good time it chose to come, was neither avoidable nor worth avoiding. In those circumstances, one might as well welcome death and have it over with.

Shakespeare was writing a stage play, not a historical record (though the differences between the two genres are neither as great as is sometimes thought, nor were they in Shakespeare's time as well defined as they are now). In terms of the historical record as he and his time knew it, however, his account is essentially accurate. His primary source was Sir Thomas North's translation (from the French, rather than from the original Greek) of Plutarch's *Lives of the Noble Greek and Romans,* dating from the end of the first century C.E. North's translation of 1579 was augmented, in the editions of 1595 and 1603, by passages drawn from a variety of other authors. No full account of how Shakespeare handled North's vigorous prose is needed, here: the two passages that follow, first North and then *Antony and Cleopatra,* provide a perfect illustration of Shakespeare at work. (In the Shakespeare passage, Caesar is speaking to Antony, reminding him of his great past exploits.)

And therefore it was a wonderful example to the soldiers, to see Antony that was brought up in all fineness and superfluity, so easily to drink puddle water, and to eat wild fruits and roots. And moreover it is reported that, even as they passed the Alps, they did eat the barks of trees, and such beasts as never man tasted of their flesh before. (normalized spelling and punctuation)

> Thou didst drink
> The stale of horses, and the gilded puddle
> Which beasts would cough at. Thy palate then did deign
> The roughest berry on the rudest hedge.
> Yea, like the stag, when snow the pasture sheets,
> The barks of trees thou browsed'st. On the Alps
> It is reported thou didst eat strange flesh,
> Which some did die to look on.
>
> (1.4.62–69)

North's robust bluntness is extremely effective. To describe a wealthy Roman aristocrat, which Antony was (indeed, his early reputation was that of a carousing playboy), being forced to drink "puddle water," is in a sense to say all that, in a work of history, needs saying (though I should add that Elizabethan streets were a great deal dirtier even than streets today). And Shakespeare's verse presentation vastly intensifies the picture. He first tells us that Antony had to drink the urine of horses. And then he adds that Antony was also obliged to drink from scum-covered pools of stagnant water that even animals could not tolerate. This is not a question, of course, of falsifying the historical record, for a dramatic re-creation and not a historical record is what Shakespeare is writing.

Further: North tells us that Antony then ate "wild fruits and roots" and, at a later point, as they "passed the Alps," ate even "the barks of trees." Not only does Shakespeare vividly amplify this but—for at least two reasons, which I shall examine in a moment—joins these two episodes into one. Antony's refined palate was expanded, remarkably, to include "the roughest berry on the rudest hedge." Note that, for Shakespeare's time, the adjective "wild" bore, in dealing with both animals and plants, the notion of inferior characteristics, just as, in dealing with lands and whole regions, "wild" meant "waste, desert, desolate." Human beings who were "wild" were, logically enough, not simply "savage" but also "uncultured, rude, uncontrolled." Orderly animals, and plants, regions, and people, were of a higher and better sort. Shakespeare and North were contemporaneous, if not precisely contemporaries, so "wild" carried more or less the same associations for both men. But for Shakespeare's purposes the plain word "wild" needed to be both particularized (into "berry") and intensified (into "the *roughest* berry"). And even the "roughest berry" had to be picked from a "hedge" (such rows of bushes and small trees were universal in Elizabethan England), and not from just any hedge, but the "rudest"—that is, the most barbarous, uncultivated, irrationally unmaintained of all.

North treats "wild fruits and roots" separately from "bark" eating, but by combining what were historically separate episodes, Shakespeare achieves still further intensification, both of "wildness" and also of the flesh-eating episode that follows. Antony is compared to a stag—wild, to be sure, but without question animal-like (the Elizabethans preferred the word "beast" to the word "animal")—perilously surviving, in bitter winter cold, by gnawing on the bark of trees. By separating the flesh-eating from the bark-eating portions, Shakespeare is able to amplify the latter—experienced on its own—as something a great deal more gruesome than merely eating the flesh of unknown animals. Antony does indeed, in Shakespeare, still eat "strange flesh," but "strange" contains vastly more possibilities for dramatic effect than that which is merely unknown. "Strange" incorporates notions of abnormality, queerness, mystery, and thus of a kind of unaccountable hostility. And Shakespeare nails this to the wall, as it were, by adding, with stunning invention, not simply that this "strange" flesh was dangerous, as North implies but does not directly state, but that it was mortally so. Worse, it could kill, like some inanimate, Medusa-like substance, simply by being seen: "which some did die to look on." Magic and superstition were perceived by the Elizabethans as far more common, and often as far more venomous, than for the most part they are today. Elizabethans would shudder, at least inwardly, at such potently lethal once-living flesh. And that was exactly what Shakespeare meant to them to do: "such beasts as never men tasted of their flesh before" was adequate for his purposes. We might say, without I think impugning Shakespeare's sense of history, that he was inventing as well as transmitting it.

Antony and Cleopatra *as Love Story*

Writers have always known that a love story, whether it ends tragically or happily, is defined as much by its setting as by its protagonists. The shabby dullness of French bourgeois life lies at the very center of Gustave Flaubert's *Madame Bovary;* Thomas Mann's *Death in Venice* pivots on the contrasts between stodgy, sane Germany and brilliant, tawdry Italy; Bernard Malamud's *The Assistant* is steeped in, and its lovers wonderfully triumph over, the harshness of big-city life in the Great Depression; and can one imagine the fairy-tale happiness of Charles Dickens' *David Copperfield* without the bustle and the misery of nineteenth-century London?

The love story that turns the plot of *Antony and Cleopatra* is hinged on the pulsing tensions between the stalwart, powerful, but corrupted existence of classical Rome and the fragrant, sensual, tropical solipsism of Egypt. It is abundantly clear, from what we learn of Antony in *Julius Caesar,* that he perfectly embodies classical Rome at its best and its worst. Though Brutus and the other conspirators against Julius Caesar do not think a pleasure-loving young aristocrat can threaten their coup d'état, Antony proves them wrong. Not only does he rise to the occasion, but together with young Octavius Caesar (and a "solid" bureaucrat, M. Aemilius Lepidus) he becomes one of the three all-powerful rulers of the then-known world. But he still so strongly embodies, as well, the decadence of Rome, which shirks civic responsibility and instead seeks luxurious enjoyment, that he is captivated, and ultimately destroyed, by the Queen of Egypt (the "Witch/Whore of the East"), voluptuous, self-centered Cleopatra. In act 1, scene 1, at lines 33–39, he declares the creed of this aspect of his being:

> Let Rome in Tiber melt, and the wide arch
> Of the rangèd empire fall! Here is my space.
> Kingdoms are clay. Our dungy earth alike
> Feeds beast as man. The nobleness of life
> Is to do thus. (*embraces Cleopatra*) When such a mutual pair
> And such a twain can do't, in which I bind
> (On pain of punishment) the world to weet
> We stand up peerless.

Like everything he does, this posture seems to Antony, as he states it—and as he enacts it—a final and inevitable truth. And by the second scene of this same first act, he utterly renounces what he has just proclaimed (and in the fulfillment of which he has for some years been living): "These strong Egyptian fetters I must break, / Or lose myself in dotage. . . . I must from this enchanting queen break off. / Ten thousand harms, more than the ills I know, / My idleness doth hatch" (lines 111–12, 123–25).

He has had exceedingly troubling letters from Rome, which only moments before he has completely refused to so much as glance at, then changes his mind, looks—and is transformed (for the nonce):

> Sextus Pompeius
> Hath given the dare to Caesar, and commands
> The empire of the sea. Our slippery people,
> Whose love is never linked to the deserver
> Till his deserts are past, begin to throw
> Pompey the Great and all his dignities
> Upon his son, who high in name and power,
> Higher than both in blood and life, stands up
> For the main soldier. Whose quality, going on,
> The sides o' the world may danger.
>
> (lines 175–84)

In short, Antony is in no way a weak man, and even less a malicious one, but he quite lacks the steady, fixated sense of purpose, and the driving need for power, that in the end inevitably cause Octavius' victory and Antony's defeated death.

Cleopatra, flitting and largely (though not completely) self-fixated as she is, nevertheless has led a relatively triumphant existence of almost fairy-tale pleasure. Not many women in her time, or in Shakespeare's, had so brilliantly, so notably succeeded in living virtually on her own terms. The highly personal power that this deeply integrated woman possesses is felt by everyone she encounters, from conquering emperors to mere servants. Nor is hers an exclusively sexual enchantment, for it is effective on women and even on a eunuch. The reluctant adoration given her by Eno- barbus, Antony's confidant, is often cited to demonstrate the reach of Cleopatra's charms—that is, of her magic, rather than her mere personality. But I find even more compelling her effect on the rather mysterious Dolabella, a trusted diplomatic agent of Caesar. Sent to cajole Cleopatra into submission, for Caesar strongly de- sires the famous queen of Egypt as an adornment to his ceremo- nial victory procession into Rome, Dolabella instead succumbs to her:

> Hear me, good madam.
> Your loss is as yourself, great, and you bear it
> As answering to the weight.
>
> . . . .
>
>   I do feel,
> By the rebound of yours, a grief that smites
> My very heart at root.
>
>   (5.2.99–101, 102–4)

Forbidden as he is to tell her the truth about Caesar's plans for her, he not only tells her but soon returns to give her precise time-and- date information. Their brief exchange is deeply revealing:

Dolabella Madam, as thereto sworn by your command,
> Which my love makes religion to obey,
> I tell you this. Caesar through Syria
> Intends his journey, and within three days
> You with your children will he send before.
> Make your best use of this. I have performed

Your pleasure, and my promise.

Cleopatra   Dolabella,

I shall remain your debtor.

Dolabella   I your servant.

Adieu good Queen, I must attend on Caesar.

Cleopatra Farewell, and thanks.

(5.2.196–204)

Although a deft and clever diplomatist—skills he proves by es-
caping scot-free, after so fundamental betrayal of his lord and
master, the usually vengeful Caesar—he here acknowledges himself bound to Cleopatra, "sworn" to her command, and so totally
dominated that his fealty is more "religion" than mere duty.

But Antony's surging, sometimes-off, sometimes-on worship
of the same deity is incredibly compelling. Falsely told (on Cleopatra's instructions: he is furious at her military betrayal) that
Cleopatra is dead, he proclaims, as passionately as distractedly:

I will o'ertake thee, Cleopatra,

And weep for my pardon. So it must be, for now

All length is torture.

. . . .

Eros! – I come, my queen – Eros! – Stay for me.

Where souls do couch on flowers, we'll hand in hand,

And with our sprightly port make the ghosts gaze.

(4.14.44–46, 50–52)

Just before he finishes the slow process of a self-inflicted death,
Antony tells Cleopatra:

I am dying, Egypt, dying. Only

I here importune death awhile, until

Of many thousand kisses the poor last
I lay upon thy lips.

(4.15.18−21)

Commenting on Cleopatra's own self-inflicted death, Robert Ornstein writes (in a remarkably perceptive and wide-ranging essay): "Part of the mystery of her death is the fulness with which it expresses the multiplicity of her nature. She is Antony's mistress and his wife, the graceful courtesan and the tender mother, the great queen and the simple lass. Her drowsiness [, here,] is at once sensual, maternal, and child-like."[6]

Antony and Cleopatra *as Tragedy*

For better or worse, this is not tragedy in its usual form. The classic model, framed by Aristotle more than two millennia ago, provides for a highly placed tragic hero, afflicted with a crucial flaw, who is brought down by that flaw. He may or may not die: the central requirement is his loss of status and rank. Hamlet clearly adheres to this classic model, though there has always been disagreement about the exact nature of his flaw. Othello also fits the model, as does Lear. But Antony only partially fits the classic model. He is highly placed, he is flawed, and he falls. On the other hand, in his long periods of voluptuous isolation he is in fact not the same highly placed Roman he has been. Indeed, in the play's very first line, spoken by Philo, one of Antony's associates, Antony is very seriously described as being in his "dotage," a kind of senility or second childhood. Philo documents his charge, and concludes the sober indictment by calling Antony "The triple pillar of the world transformed / Into a strumpet's fool" (1.1.12−13). Can the collapse of a "fool" be termed either heroic or tragic?

Of course, Antony is not always "a strumpet's fool," and without question he dies heroically. On the other hand, his death is perhaps more a triumph than a fall—a reassertion of who and what, at his best, he is capable of being. And that "best" is as a lover quite as much as an emperor. ("In one sense, *Antony and Cleopatra* is actionless. A world is lost, but it is so well lost that it seems not to have been lost at all; its immensity was not disturbed.")[7] As Antony tells Cleopatra, in almost his last words:

> The miserable change now at my end
> Lament nor sorrow at. But please your thoughts
> In feeding them with those my former fortunes
> Wherein I lived. The greatest prince o' the world,
> The noblest.
>
> (4.15.51–55)

"The miserable change," here, can be viewed as both the fall in his fortunes and the quite literal "change" in his way of life. In short, like so much about this play, Antony as a tragic hero is forever somewhat ambiguous.

Cleopatra, who loses her lover, her throne, and her life, is just as powerfully one of the protagonists in a tragedy. She is arguably less exalted—noble by birth and by consecration as a queen, but rather less than "noble" throughout much of her life. She is exceedingly vain, which is of course forgivable. She is frequently a liar, which is forgivable. She is inclined to treachery, when she thinks it necessary, which is forgivable. She is capable of being paralyzed by fear (as in act 4, scene 15, when she is afraid to descend to the dying Antony, or when earlier she sails away in sheer terror of actual wartime confrontation, turning her flagship vessel into a signal for surrender), which is forgivable. She is sometimes savage and cruel, which is forgivable. She remains the great Cleopatra, in short, but the great Cleopatra is far from unambiguously great.

And if Antony's fall is in some degree a triumph, what are we to say of Cleopatra, whose death scene is one of the most magnificent, virtuosic ascensions to the heights in all of literature? ("[Antony and Cleopatra] prefer each other's untruth to any truth that has yet to be tried. This does not make them easy material for tragedy. It makes them indeed the most intractable material of all; for tragedy works with delusions, and they have none.")[8] Cleopatra's last appearance does not begin, as do many of the heroic scenes in this and others of Shakespeare's plays, with a blasting trumpet call. But her opening words might serve as a sounding trumpet: "Give me my robe, put on my crown, I have / Immortal longings in me." Immortality is hardly a lesser state, no matter how high one stands. She goes on:

> Methinks I hear
> Antony call. I see him rouse himself
> To praise my noble act. I hear him mock
> The luck of Caesar, which the gods give men
> To excuse their after wrath. Husband, I come.
> Now to that name my courage prove my title.
> I am fire, and air, my other elements
> I give to baser life.

> (5.2.278–85)

Once Cleopatra has set the poisonous asp at her breast, Charmian cries out—and Cleopatra's response, though still triumphant, is now maternal as well:

> Peace, peace.
> Dost thou not see my baby at my breast,
> That sucks the nurse asleep?
>
> (5.2.303–5)

Rather than seeing herself as the "victim" of a poisonous snake, Cleopatra here turns herself into the giver, not the recipient, and what she gives is, metaphorically, life rather than death. The play has indeed become "an ecstasy in which the power of imagination has taken over the world and the world lives only in the power of imagination."[9]

Yet there is still more to the complexity of this play's tragic dimensions. Enobarbus, one of the secondary characters, has so strongly delineated a character, is so much at the center of the action, and is both so clearly noble and, in the end, has so clearly fallen, that it is tempting to consider him, too, as part of this play's complex and unresolvable tragedy. Enobarbus is depicted as fiercely loyal to Antony, but the historical Domitius Ahenobarbus, from a famous noble family, did not clearly ally himself with Antony until after the Treaty of Brundisium (40 B.C.E.), framed by Octavius Caesar and Antony to establish peace between one another. His decision to leave Antony's camp, and go over to Caesar's, is portrayed as exceedingly difficult and made only after long, troubled thought:

> When valor preys on reason,
> It eats the sword it fights with. I will seek
> Some way to leave him
>
> (3.13.198–200)

Having deserted his longtime friend and master, he remains un-satisfied: "I have done ill, / Of which I do accuse myself so sorely / That I will joy no more" (4.6.17–19). He is told that Antony, far from being angry, retains his affection for Enobarbus and not only returns his abandoned treasure chest to him but adds a "bounty overplus," a generous parting gift. Enobarbus has learned that Caesar intends to use him, as well as other deserters, in battle against Antony. Hearing of Antony's loving munificence, his spirit falls, and his life with it:

> I am alone the villain of the earth,
> And feel I am so most. O Antony,
> Thou mine of bounty, how wouldst thou have paid
> My better service, when my turpitude
> Thou dost so crown with gold! This blows my heart,
> If swift thought break it not. A swifter mean
> Shall outstrike thought, but thought will do't, I feel.
> I fight against thee? No, I will go seek
> Some ditch wherein to die. The foul'st best fits
> My latter part of life.
>
> (4.6.29–38)

If not so large a tragedy as those involving Antony and Cleopatra, Shakespeare has nevertheless made this genuinely tragic. We feel a deep respect for Enobarbus. His Roman heritage has led him astray, he has erred, and he dies. How better to define tragedy?

There is, in fact, both tragedy and triumph (of one sort or an-other) all across the vast extent of this majestic play. "This is a cu-rious play," observes Rosalie L. Colie, "resting on an ambivalent concept of love impossible to sum up, to categorize, or to de-fine. . . . In the *ping* and *pong* of plain and grandiloquent styles, now one seeming to lead and now the other, Shakespeare manages to show us the problem and the problematics, in moral as in literary terms, at the heart of style."[10] I do not think either the magical impact or the ambivalent working out of that impact can be better phrased.

Notes

1. Mark Van Doren, *Shakespeare* (New York: Holt, 1939), 230; Alvin Kernan, *Shakespeare, the King's Playwright: Theater in the Stuart Court, 1603–1613* (New Haven and London: Yale University Press, 1995), 123; Harold C. Goddard, *The Meaning of Shakespeare,* 2 vols. (Chicago: University of Chicago Press, 1951), 2:184.

2. Van Doren, *Shakespeare,* 232.

3. David Grene, *The Actor in History: Studies in Shakespearean Stage Poetry* (University Park: Pennsylvania State University Press, 1988), 13.

4. Douglas Bush, *Prefaces to Renaissance Literature* (New York: W. W. Norton, 1965), 11.

5. G. Gregory Smith, ed., *Elizabethan Critical Essays,* 2 vols. (Oxford: Clarendon Press, 1904), 1:5.

6. Robert Ornstein, "The Ethic of the Imagination: Love and Art in *Antony and Cleopatra,*" in Leonard F. Dean, ed., *Shakespeare: Modern Essays in Criticism,* rev. ed. (New York: Oxford University Press, 1967), 401.

7. Van Doren, *Shakespeare,* 236.

8. Ibid., 239.

9. Grene, *Actor in History,* 17.

10. Rosalie L. Colie, *Shakespeare's Living Art* (Princeton, N.J.: Princeton University Press, 1974), 204, 207.

SOME ESSENTIALS OF THE
SHAKESPEAREAN STAGE

The Stage

- There was no *scenery* (backdrops, flats, and so on).

- Compared to today's elaborate, high-tech productions, the Elizabethan stage had few *on-stage* props. These were mostly handheld: a sword or dagger, a torch or candle, a cup or flask. Larger props, such as furniture, were used sparingly.

- Costumes (some of which were upper-class castoffs, belonging to the individual actors) were elaborate. As in most premodern and very hierarchical societies, clothing was the distinctive mark of who and what a person was.

- What the actors *spoke,* accordingly, contained both the dramatic and narrative material we have come to expect in a theater (or movie house) and (1) the setting, including details of the time of day, the weather, and so on, and (2) the occasion. The *dramaturgy* is thus very different from that of our own time, requiring much more attention to verbal and gestural matters. Strict realism was neither intended nor, under the circumstances, possible.

- There was *no curtain*. Actors entered and left via doors in the back of the stage, behind which was the "tiring-room," where actors put on or changed their costumes.

- In *public theaters* (which were open-air structures), there was no *lighting;* performances could take place only in daylight hours.

- For *private* theaters, located in large halls of aristocratic houses, candlelight illumination was possible.

The Actors

- Actors worked in *professional,* for-profit companies, sometimes organized and owned by other actors, and sometimes by entrepreneurs who could afford to erect or rent the company's building. Public theaters could hold, on average, two thousand playgoers, most of whom viewed and listened while standing. Significant profits could be and were made. Private theaters were smaller, more exclusive.

- There was *no director.* A book-holder/prompter/props manager, standing in the tiring-room behind the backstage doors, worked from a text marked with entrances and exits and notations of any special effects required for that particular script. A few such books have survived. Actors had texts only of their own parts, speeches being cued to a few prior words. There were few and often no rehearsals, in our modern use of the term, though there was often some coaching of individuals. Since Shakespeare's England was largely an oral culture, actors learned their parts rapidly and retained them for years. This was *repertory* theater, repeating popular plays and introducing some new ones each season.

- *Women* were not permitted on the professional stage. Most female roles were acted by *boys;* elderly women were played by grown men.

The Audience

- London's professional theater operated in what might be called a "red-light" district, featuring brothels, restaurants, and the kind of *open-air entertainment* then most popular, like bear-baiting (in which a bear, tied to a stake, was set on by dogs).

- A theater audience, like most of the population of Shakespeare's England, was largely made up of *illiterates.* Being able to read and write, however, had nothing to do with intelligence or concern with language, narrative, and characterization. People attracted to the theater tended to be both extremely verbal and extremely volatile. Actors were sometimes attacked, when the audience was dissatisfied; quarrels and fights were relatively common. Women were regularly in attendance, though no reliable statistics exist.

- Drama did not have the cultural esteem it has in our time, and plays were not regularly printed. Shakespeare's often appeared in book form, but not with any supervision or other involvement on his part. He wrote a good deal of nondramatic poetry as well, yet so far as we know he did not authorize or supervise *any* work of his that appeared in print during his lifetime.

- Playgoers, who had paid good money to see and hear, plainly gave dramatic performances careful, detailed attention. For some closer examination of such matters, see Burton Raffel, "Who Heard the Rhymes and How: Shakespeare's Dramaturgical Signals," *Oral Tradition* 11 (October 1996): 190–221, and Raffel, "Metrical Dramaturgy in Shakespeare's Earlier Plays," *CEA Critic* 57 (Spring–Summer 1995): 51–65.

Antony and Cleopatra

CHARACTERS (DRAMATIS PERSONAE)

Mark Antony, Octavius Caesar, M. Aemilius Lepidus (triumvirs)[1]

Sextus Pompeius, Domitius Enobarbus, Ventidius, Eros, Scarus,
   Decretas, Demetrius, Philo (Antony's friends)

Maecenas, Agrippa, Dolabella, Proculeius, Thidias, Gallus (Caesar's
   friends)

Menas, Menecrates, Varrius (Pompey's friends)

Taurus (Caesar's lieutenant general)

Canidius (Antony's lieutenant general)

Silius (officer in Ventidius' army)

Euphronius (Antony's ambassador to Caesar)

Alexas, Mardian, Seleucus, Diomedes (Cleopatra's male attendants)

Soothsayer, Rustic

Cleopatra (Queen of Egypt)

Octavia (Caesar's sister and Antony's wife)

Charmian, Iras (Cleopatra's female attendants)

Officers, Soldiers, Messengers, and other Attendants

1 the three joint leaders of Rome, in theory of equal power

Act I

Alexandria, a room in Cleopatra's palace

ENTER DEMETRIUS AND PHILO

Philo Nay, but this dotage[1] of our general's[2]
  O'erflows the measure.[3] Those his goodly[4] eyes
  That o'er the files and musters[5] of the war
  Have glowed like plated[6] Mars, now bend, now turn
  The office[7] and devotion of their view   5
  Upon[8] a tawny front.[9] His captain's[10] heart,

1 second childhood, senility
2 Antony
3 o'erflows the measure = (*literally*) exceeds the capacity of the measuring
  instrument / the standard by which such matters are judged, (*colloquially*) is
  simply too much / beyond all tolerance
4 excellent, admirable, highly capable
5 files and musters = lists / rolls / records and inspections / reviews of manpower
6 armor-plated
7 attention, duty, business★
8 on, toward
9 face (i.e., Cleopatra)
10 captain's = leader's, general's (as still used in "captains of industry")★

3

Which in the scuffles[11] of great fights hath burst
The buckles on his breast,[12] reneges[13] all temper,[14]
And is become the bellows[15] and the fan
To cool a gypsy's[16] lust.

FLOURISH[17]

ENTER ANTONY, CLEOPATRA, WITH HER ATTENDANTS
AND WITH EUNUCHS FANNING HER

10   Look where they come.
Take but good note, and you shall see in him
The triple pillar[18] of the world transformed
Into a strumpet's[19] fool. Behold and see.

Cleopatra If it be love indeed,[20] tell me how much.

15 *Antony* There's beggary[21] in the love that can be reckoned.[22]

Cleopatra I'll set a bourn[23] how far to be beloved.

Antony Then must thou needs find out new heaven, new
earth.

ENTER ATTENDANT

11 scrambling combat
12 burst the buckles on his breast: metaphoric
13 renounces, abandons, deserts
14 balance, regulation
15 i.e., oxygen-supplying mechanism for assorted passions/fires
16 the dark-skinned people known as gypsies were thought to come from
   Egypt, Cleopatra's country
17 fanfare*
18 triple pillar = one of three props/supports ("triumvirs")
19 harlot's, whore's
20 truly, in fact
21 extreme poverty
22 counted up, recited, evaluated
23 boundary, limit

Attendant News,[24] my good lord, from Rome.

Antony   Grates[25] me. The

   sum.[26]

Cleopatra Nay, hear them,[27] Antony:

   Fulvia[28] perchance is angry. Or who knows   20

   If the scarce-bearded[29] Caesar have not sent

   His powerful mandate[30] to you, "Do this, or this,

   Take in[31] that kingdom, and enfranchise[32] that,

   Perform 't, or else we damn[33] thee."

Antony   How, my love?

Cleopatra Perchance?[34] Nay, and most like.[35]   25

   You must not stay here longer, your dismission[36]

   Is[37] come from Caesar, therefore hear it, Antony.

   Where's Fulvia's process?[38] Caesar's, I would say?[39] Both?

   Call in the messengers. As I am Egypt's queen,

   Thou blushest, Antony; and that blood of thine   30

24 brought by the messengers later noted
25 irritates
26 the sum = let me hear it in summary/a few words
27 (1) the news, which was in Shakespeare's time considered a plural noun, *or*
   (2) the messengers
28 Antony's wife, d. 40 B.C.E., after which Antony, temporarily reconciled with
   Octavius Caesar, married Octavia, Caesar's sister
29 i.e., very young
30 order, injunction, command
31 capture, absorb
32 free
33 condemn, denounce
34 perhaps
35 likely, probably
36 deprivation of/dismissal from office
37 has
38 suit, summons, writ
39 I would say = that is

Is Caesar's homager.[40] Else so[41] thy cheek pays[42] shame

When shrill-tongued Fulvia scolds. The messengers!

Antony   Let Rome in Tiber[43] melt, and the wide arch[44]

Of the rangèd[45] empire fall! Here is my space.[46]

35   Kingdoms are clay.[47] Our dungy[48] earth alike[49]

Feeds beast as[50] man. The nobleness of life

Is to do thus. (*embraces her*) When such a mutual pair[51]

And such a twain[52] can do't, in[53] which I bind[54]

(On pain of punishment)[55] the world to weet[56]

We stand up peerless.[57]

40   *Cleopatra*   Excellent falsehood.

Why did he marry Fulvia, and not[58] love her?

I'll seem the fool I am not. Antony

Will be himself.

Antony   But stirred by Cleopatra.

---

40 Caesar's homager = your act of fealty/homage to Caesar
41 else so = were it otherwise★
42 cheek pays = face★ is covered with
43 the river Tiber, which flows through Rome
44 arch: in the sense of a support structure
45 ordered, systematically arranged
46 proper place/location
47 earth ("mere" earth)
48 DUNGee: composed of dung, dirt
49 equally, in the same manner
50 as it does
51 mutual pair = reciprocal/intimate set of two
52 two separate parts/persons
53 as to
54 oblige, require
55 i.e., the world will be punished if it does not "weet"
56 understand ("wit")
57 stand up peerless = remain unequaled/matchless
58 and not = if he did not

Now, for the love of Love,[59] and her[60] soft hours,

Let's not confound[61] the time with conference[62] harsh.   45

There's not a minute of our lives should stretch[63]

Without some pleasure now. What sport[64] tonight?

Cleopatra Hear the ambassadors.

Antony   Fie, wrangling[65] queen!

Whom everything becomes,[66] to chide,[67] to laugh,

To weep, whose every passion[68] fully strives   50

To make itself, in thee, fair[69] and admired![70]

No messenger, but thine, and all alone

Tonight we'll wander through the streets and note[71]

The qualities[72] of people. Come, my queen.

Last night you did desire it. (*to Messengers*) Speak not to us.   55

EXEUNT[73] ANTONY AND CLEOPATRA AND ATTENDANTS

Demetrius Is Caesar with Antonius prized[74] so slight?

Philo   Sir, sometimes, when he is not Antony,

He comes too short of that great property[75]

59 Venus, the goddess of Love
60 Love's
61 ruin, destroy, defeat★
62 discourse, talk ("conversation")
63 extend, flow, go forward
64 entertainment, amusement, diversion
65 quarreling
66 graces, suits
67 scold★
68 emotion★
69 beautiful★
70 wondered at★
71 observe★
72 characters, natures
73 plural form of "exit"
74 valued, esteemed
75 condition, state

Which still[76] should go with[77] Antony.
60 *Demetrius* I am full sorry
That he approves[78] the common liar, who
Thus speaks of him at Rome. But I will hope
Of[79] better deeds tomorrow. Rest you happy!

EXEUNT

76 always
77 with being
78 demonstrates/proves the truthfulness of
79 for

SCENE 2

Alexandria, Cleopatra's palace, another room

ENTER CHARMIAN,[1] DOMITIUS ENOBARBUS,[2]
IRAS,[3] ALEXAS, AND SOOTHSAYER

Charmian Lord Alexas, sweet Alexas, most anything Alexas,
almost most absolute[4] Alexas, where's the soothsayer that you
praised so to the Queen? O that I knew this husband,[5]
which, you say, must charge[6] his horns with garlands![7]

Alexas   Soothsayer.   5

Soothsayer Your will?

Charmian Is this the man? Is't you, sir, that know things?

Soothsayer In nature's infinite book of secrecy
A little I can read.

Alexas   Show him your hand.[8]

Enobarbus Bring in the banquet[9] quickly; wine enough   10
Cleopatra's health to drink.

Charmian Good sir, give me good fortune.

Soothsayer I make not, but foresee.

Charmian Pray then, foresee me one.

Soothsayer You shall be yet far fairer than you are.   15

Charmian He means in flesh.[10]

---

1 KARmeeun
2 doMEEshus enoBARbus
3 EARahs
4 perfect, complete
5 i.e., a possible / future husband for her
6 Folio: change; most editors emend
7 charge his horns with garlands = loan his cuckold's horns with cheerful
  decorations (i.e., not be troubled when his wife – Charmian – cuckolds him)
8 palm (to be read)
9 fruit and wine (i.e., light food and drink)
10 have an excess of flesh ("plumper")

Iras	No, you shall paint[11] when you are old.
Charmian	Wrinkles forbid!
Alexas	Vex[12] not his prescience,[13] be attentive.
20 *Charmian*	Hush!
Soothsayer	You shall be more beloving[14] than beloved.
Charmian	I had rather heat my liver[15] with drinking.
Alexas	Nay, hear him.

Charmian Good now, some excellent fortune! Let me be
25 married to three kings in a forenoon,[16] and widow[17] them
all. Let me have a child at fifty, to whom Herod[18] of Jewry
may do homage. Find me[19] to marry me with Octavius
Caesar, and companion me[20] with my mistress.

Soothsayer You shall outlive the lady whom you serve.

30 *Charmian* O excellent! I love long life better than figs.

Soothsayer You have seen and proved[21] a fairer former fortune
Than that which is to approach.

Charmian Then belike[22] my children shall have no names.[23]
Prithee,[24] how many boys and wenches[25] must I have?

35 *Soothsayer* If every of your wishes had a womb,

11 use cosmetics (then considered not entirely proper)
12 harass, trouble, annoy
13 divine foreknowledge
14 loving
15 regarded as the center of love and passion
16 before noon
17 become the widow of
18 Herod was the Roman ruler/king of Judea (see Matt. 2:1–16)
19 fined me = discover that I am to
20 companion me = let me be companion
21 attested to, proven genuine
22 probably★
23 i.e., be bastards
24 I pray you ("please")★
25 girls, women★

And fertile every wish, a million.

Charmian Out[26] fool! I forgive thee for[27] a witch.

Alexas You think none but your sheets are privy to[28] your wishes.

Charmian Nay, come, tell Iras hers.   40

Alexas We'll know all[29] our fortunes.

Enobarbus Mine, and most of our fortunes tonight, shall be – drunk[30] to bed.

Iras There's a palm presages[31] chastity, if nothing else.

Charmian E'en as the o'erflowing Nilus presageth famine.[32]   45

Iras (*to Charmian*) Go, you wild bedfellow, you cannot soothsay.

Charmian Nay, if an oily palm[33] be not a fruitful prognostication, I cannot scratch mine ear. Prithee, tell her but a worky-day[34] fortune.   50

Soothsayer Your fortunes are alike.

Iras But how, but how? Give me particulars.

Soothsayer I have said.[35]

Iras Am I not an inch of fortune better than she?

Charmian Well, if you were but an inch of fortune better than I,   55
where would you choose it?[36]

---

26 exclamation of indignation / reproach
27 because you are after all
28 privy to = familiar with
29 we'll know all = we all wish to know
30 to go drunk
31 predicts, augurs
32 not on your life (i.e., the overflowing Nile★ means a good harvest, not famine)
33 a damp / moist palm predicted wantonness
34 workaday ("ordinary, common")
35 spoken
36 choose it = choose it to be

Iras   Not in my husband's nose.[37]

Charmian Our worser thoughts heavens mend![38] Alexas –
come, his fortune, his fortune! O, let him marry a woman that
60   cannot go,[39] sweet Isis,[40] I beseech thee! And let her die too,
and give him a worse! And let worst follow worse, till the
worst of all follow him laughing to his grave, fifty-fold a
cuckold! Good Isis, hear me this prayer, though thou deny
me a matter of more weight. Good Isis, I beseech thee!

65 *Iras*   Amen, dear goddess, hear that prayer of the people!
For as it is a heartbreaking to see a handsome man loose-
wived,[41] so it is a deadly sorrow to behold a foul knave[42]
uncuckolded. Therefore dear Isis, keep decorum,[43] and
fortune him accordingly!

70 *Charmian* Amen.

Alexas   Lo now, if it lay in their hands to make me a cuckold,
they would make themselves whores, but they'd do't!

Enobarbus Hush, here comes Antony.

Charmian Not he, the Queen.

ENTER CLEOPATRA

Cleopatra Saw you my lord?

Enobarbus   No, lady.

75 *Cleopatra*   Was he not here?

Charmian No, madam.

---

37 by implication, in his genitals
38 heavens mend = may the heavens improve/reform★
39 (?) have an orgasm
40 goddess of female fertility (EYEsis)
41 with a wife behaving wantonly/immorally
42 foul knave = loathsome/offensive★ base fellow/rascal★
43 keep decorum = preserve★ propriety★

Cleopatra He was disposed to[44] mirth, but on the sudden
    A Roman thought hath struck him. Enobarbus!
Enobarbus Madam.
Cleopatra Seek him, and bring him hither. Where's Alexas?   80
Alexas Here at your service. My lord approaches.
Cleopatra We will not look upon him. Go with us.

EXEUNT

ENTER MARK ANTONY WITH A MESSENGER
AND ATTENDANTS

Antony Against my brother Lucius?
Messenger Ay.
    But soon that war had end, and the time's state[46]   85
    Made friends of them, joining their force 'gainst Caesar,
    Whose better issue[47] in the war, from Italy
    Upon[48] the first encounter drave[49] them.
Antony Well, what worst?
Messenger The nature of bad news infects[50] the teller.   90
Antony When it concerns the fool or coward. On.[51]
    Things that are past are done with me. 'Tis thus:
    Who tells me true, though in his tale lie death,
    I hear him as[52] he flattered.

---

44 disposed to = in the mood for
45 i.e., she engaged in open conflict with first Lucius Antony (Mark Antony's
    brother) and then, together with Lucius, against Augustus Caesar
46 the time's state = the state / condition of the time
47 result
48 at
49 encounter drave = battle defeated
50 stains, taints
51 continue, go on
52 as if

Messenger   Labienus[53] –

95   This is stiff[54] news – hath, with his Parthian force,

Extended Asia from Euphrates.[55]

His conquering banner shook from Syria

To Lydia[56] and to Ionia,[57] whilst – (*he pauses*)

Antony   Antony, thou wouldst[58] say.

Messenger   O my lord.

100 Antony   Speak to me home,[59] mince[60] not the general

tongue,[61]

Name Cleopatra as she is called in Rome.

Rail[62] thou in Fulvia's phrase, and taunt my faults

With such full license as both truth and malice

Have power to utter. O then we bring forth weeds,

105   When our quick winds[63] lie still, and our ills told[64] us

Is as our earing.[65] Fare thee well awhile.

Messenger At your noble pleasure.

EXIT MESSENGER

Antony   From Sicion[66] how the news? Speak there.

53 anti-triumvir general, allied with local Parthians (Greek-Persian) against
   Antony (laBEEunus)
54 difficult, hard, formidable
55 great Middle Eastern river (youFREIGHTeez)
56 Persian-dominated kingdom
57 Middle Eastern Greek-Persian kingdom
58 wish to
59 directly, forcefully
60 moderate, make light of
61 general tongue = common/universal comments
62 curse, scold
63 quick winds = lively★ seed-bearing forces
64 when told to
65 ploughing★ our fields
66 Sicion (SIseeun): Greek city-state W of Athens and E of Corinth

Attendant 1 (*calling*) The man from Sicion. Is there such an one?

Attendant 2 He stays[67] upon your will.

Antony   Let him appear.   110
    These strong Egyptian fetters[68] I must break,
    Or lose myself in dotage.[69]

ENTER MESSENGER 2

                                    What are you?[70]

Messenger 2 Fulvia thy wife is dead.

Antony   Where died she?

Messenger 2 In Sicion.
    Her length of sickness, with what else more serious   115
    Importeth[71] thee to know, this (*gives a letter*) bears.

Antony   Forbear
    me.[72]

EXIT MESSENGERS

    There's a great spirit gone! Thus did I desire it.
    What our contempt doth often hurl[73] from us,
    We wish it ours again. The present[74] pleasure,
    By revolution low'ring,[75] does become   120
    The opposite of itself. She's good, being gone.

67 waits
68 shackles
69 senility
70 what are you = who are you, why are you here
71 it is important for
72 forbear me = bear with me, excuse★ me
73 drive, dash, cast
74 current, immediate, instant★
75 revolution low'ring = moving/proceeding downward in its course/orbit

The hand[76] could pluck[77] her back that shoved her on.
I must from this enchanting[78] queen break off.
Ten thousand harms, more than the ills I know,
125   My idleness doth hatch. How now,[79] Enobarbus!

ENTER ENOBARBUS

Enobarbus   What's your pleasure, sir?
Antony   I must with haste from hence.
Enobarbus   Why then[80] we kill all our women. We see how
       mortal[81] an unkindness is to them. If they suffer[82] our
130   departure, death's the word.
Antony   I must be gone.
Enobarbus   Under[83] a compelling occasion, let women die. It
       were pity to cast them away for nothing, though between
       them and a great cause, they should be esteemed[84] nothing.
135   Cleopatra, catching but the least noise[85] of this, dies instantly.
       I have seen her die twenty times upon far poorer moment.[86]
       I do think there is mettle[87] in death, which commits[88] some
       loving act upon her, she hath such a celerity[89] in dying.

76 the hand = and the hand
77 pull, draw
78 (1) charming, (2) magic-making
79 how now = what ho
80 thus, under such circumstances
81 fatal
82 (1) endure, undergo, experience, (2) submit to, tolerate, allow★
83 in connection with, with reference to
84 valued at
85 rumor, talk
86 circumstances, causes
87 vigor, spirit
88 consigns, gives, performs
89 quickness, speed

Antony   She is cunning[90] past man's thought.

Enobarbus   Alack[91] sir, no, her passions are made of nothing but   140
the finest part[92] of pure love. We cannot call her winds and
waters sighs and tears. They are greater storms and tempests
than almanacs[93] can report.[94] This cannot be cunning in her.
If it be, she makes a shower of rain as well as Jove.

Antony   Would I had never seen her.   145

Enobarbus   O sir, you had then left unseen a wonderful piece of
work, which not to have been blest withal would have
discredited[95] your travel.

Antony   Fulvia is dead.

Enobarbus   Sir?   150

Antony   Fulvia is dead.

Enobarbus   Fulvia?

Antony   Dead.

Enobarbus   Why sir, give the gods a thankful sacrifice. When it
pleaseth their deities to take the wife of a man from him, it   155
shows to man the tailors of the earth, comforting therein[96]
that when old robes[97] are worn out, there are members[98] to
make new.[99] If there were no more women but Fulvia, then
had you indeed a cut,[100] and the case to be lamented. This

90 (1) dexterous, skillful, clever,★ (2) possessing magical/conjuring skills, (3) sly
91 alas★
92 portion, essence
93 annually compiled book, containing a calendar with astronomical,
astrological, and meteorological data
94 describe, give an account of
95 destroyed confidence in, lessened the value of
96 in that circumstance
97 garments
98 individuals
99 new ones
100 stroke, blow

160   grief is crowned with consolation, your old smock[101] brings
       forth a new petticoat,[102] and indeed the tears live[103] in an
       onion that should[104] water this sorrow.

   Antony   The business she hath broached[105] in the state
       Cannot endure my absence.

165 *Enobarbus* And the business you have broached here cannot be
       without you, specially that of Cleopatra's, which wholly
       depends on your abode.[106]

   Antony   No more light[107] answers. Let our[108] officers
       Have notice what we purpose.[109] I shall break[110]

170   The cause of our expedience[111] to the Queen,
       And get her leave[112] to part. For not alone
       The death of Fulvia, with more urgent touches,[113]
       Do strongly speak to us, but the letters too
       Of many our contriving[114] friends in Rome

175   Petition[115] us at[116] home. Sextus Pompeius[117]

---

101 loosely draped garment
102 waistcoat, short jacket/coat
103 reside, can be found
104 must, will
105 started, caused
106 residence, stay
107 trivial, slight, frivolous
108 the royal "we," meaning "me," Antony
109 intend★
110 reveal
111 haste
112 consent
113 matters, concerns
114 plotting, scheming, conspiring
115 solicit, ask, require
116 to be at
117 Pompey (67–36 B.C.E.), younger son of Pompey the Great (106–48 B.C.E.),
     like his father both powerful and at odds with those still more powerful★

Hath given the dare to Caesar, and commands
The empire of the sea. Our slippery people,[118]
Whose love is never linked to the deserver
Till his deserts are past, begin to throw
Pompey[119] the Great and all his dignities   180
Upon his son, who high in name and power,
Higher than both in blood and life,[120] stands up[121]
For the main[122] soldier. Whose quality,[123] going on,[124]
The sides[125] o' the world may danger.[126] Much is breeding
Which, like the courser's hair,[127] hath yet but[128] life,   185
And not a serpent's poison. Say our pleasure,
To such whose place[129] is under us, requires
Our quick remove from hence.
Enobarbus   I shall do't.

EXEUNT

118 slippery people = unstable, fickle citizens
119 POMpee★
120 blood and life = passion and vitality
121 stands up = holds/presents himself, takes on the role of
122 mightiest, most powerful/important
123 (1) capacity, skill, (2) nature, character
124 advancing, growing
125 structure ("walls")
126 endanger
127 courser's hair = hair from a horse's tail, thought to grow into a serpent if
     set in water
128 yet but = still only
129 position, rank★

SCENE 3

Cleopatra's palace, another room

ENTER CLEOPATRA, CHARMIAN, IRAS, AND ALEXAS

Cleopatra Where is he?

Charmian I did not see him since.[1]

Cleopatra (*to Alexas*) See where he is, who's with him, what he
    does.

    I did not send you.[2] If you find him sad,[3]

5   Say I am dancing. If in mirth, report

    That I am sudden sick. Quick, and return.

EXIT ALEXAS

Charmian Madam, methinks[4] if you did love him dearly,

    You do not hold the method to enforce[5]

    The like from him.

Cleopatra   What should I do, I[6] do not?

10 *Charmian* In each thing give him way, cross[7] him nothing.

Cleopatra Thou teachest like a fool. The way to lose him!

Charmian Tempt[8] him not so too far. I wish,[9] forbear.

    In time we hate[10] that which we often fear.[11]

---

1 recently
2 i.e., do not say that you were sent by me
3 (1) weary, (2) grave, serious, (3) sorrowful
4 it seems to me
5 hold the method to enforce = maintain/sustain/keep the procedure to
  urge★
6 that I
7 oppose, obstruct
8 test
9 I wish = I wish you would
10 come to hate
11 often fear = over and over have feared

But here comes Antony.

ENTER MARK ANTONY

Cleopatra   I am sick and sullen.

Antony   I am sorry to give breathing[12] to my purpose[13] –   15

Cleopatra Help me away, dear Charmian, I shall fall,

It cannot be thus long, the sides of nature[14]

Will not sustain it.

Antony   Now, my dearest queen –

Cleopatra Pray you, stand further from me.

Antony   What's the matter?

Cleopatra I know, by that same eye, there's some good news.   20

What, says the married woman you may go?

Would she had never given you leave to come!

Let her not say 'tis I that keep you here,

I have no power upon you. Hers you are.

Antony   The gods best know –

Cleopatra   O never was there queen   25

So mightily betrayed! Yet[15] at the first

I saw the treasons planted.[16]

Antony   Cleopatra –

Cleopatra Why should I think you can be mine and true,

Though you in swearing shake[17] the thronèd gods,

Who[18] have been false to Fulvia? Riotous[19] madness,   30

12 words
13 intention
14 sides of nature = human body
15 even
16 inserted, set in place
17 you shake (by much evoking)
18 you who
19 extravagant, wanton★

To be entangled with those mouth-made vows,
Which break themselves in swearing!

Antony   Most sweet queen –

Cleopatra Nay pray you seek no color[20] for your going,
But bid farewell, and go. When you sued[21] staying,

35 Then was the time for words. No going then,
Eternity was in our lips, and eyes,
Bliss in our brows' bent.[22] None our parts[23] so poor,[24]
But was a race of[25] heaven. They are so still,
Or thou, the greatest soldier of the world,
Art turned the greatest liar.

40 *Antony*   How now, lady!

Cleopatra I would I had thy inches,[26] thou shouldst know
There were[27] a heart in Egypt.[28]

Antony   Hear me, Queen.

The strong necessity of time commands
Our[29] services awhile. But my full[30] heart

45 Remains in use[31] with you. Our Italy
Shines o'er with civil swords.[32] Sextus Pompeius
Makes his approaches to the port of Rome,

20 excuse, pretext
21 pursued, begged for★
22 (noun) (1) inclination, disposition, determination, (2) cast, arch
23 qualities, character, conduct
24 BLISS in our BROWS bent NONE our PARTS so POOR
25 kind, species
26 size
27 was (conditional subjunctive)
28 the ruler *being* the land ruled, "Egypt" here means "Cleopatra"★
29 my
30 complete, entire
31 in use = tied to, occupied with (with a sexual coloring)
32 shines o'er with civil swords = glitters with the raised swords of civil war

Equality of two domestic powers
Breed scrupulous faction.[33] The hated, grown to strength,
Are newly grown to love.[34] The condemned Pompey,   50
Rich in his father's honor, creeps apace[35]
Into the hearts of such as have not thrived
Upon[36] the present state, whose numbers threaten,[37]
And quietness, grown sick of rest, would purge[38]
By any desperate change. My more particular,[39]   55
And that which most with you should safe my going,
Is Fulvia's death.

Cleopatra Though age from folly could not give me freedom,
It does from childishness. Can Fulvia die?

Antony   She's dead, my queen. (*handing her letters*)   60
Look here, and at thy sovereign[40] leisure read
The garboils[41] she awaked. At the last, best,[42]
See when and where she died.

Cleopatra   O most false love![43]
Where be the sacred vials thou shouldst fill
With sorrowful water?[44] Now I see, I see,   65
In Fulvia's death, how mine received shall be.

Antony   Quarrel no more, but be prepared to know

33 breed scrupulous faction = breeds mistrustful/hesitant dissension
34 to love = into being loved
35 quickly★
36 thrived upon = prospered★ under
37 are threatening
38 would purge = wishes/would like/prefer to cleanse/clear away★
39 personal/private motivation
40 supreme★
41 confusions, brawls, tumult★
42 and the best of all
43 i.e., Antony's for Fulvia
44 i.e., tears of mourning

The purposes I bear, which are, or cease,[45]
As you shall give the advice.[46] By the fire[47]
70   That quickens Nilus' slime,[48] I go from hence
Thy soldier, servant, making peace or war
As thou affect'st.[49]

Cleopatra   Cut my lace,[50] Charmian, come.
But let it be, I am quickly ill, and well,
So[51] Antony loves.

Antony   My precious queen, forbear,
75   And give true evidence[52] to his love, which stands[53]
An honorable[54] trial.

Cleopatra   So Fulvia told me.
I prithee, turn aside and weep for her,
Then bid adieu to me, and say the tears
Belong to Egypt. Good now,[55] play one scene
80   Of excellent dissembling, and let it look
Like perfect honor.

Antony   You'll heat my blood. No more.

Cleopatra   You can do better yet. But this is meetly.[56]

Antony   Now by my sword —

---

45 which are, or cease = which either will come to pass, or will be aborted
46 judgment, opinion
47 sun
48 quickens Nilus' slime = animates/gives life to the Nile's mud
49 prefer
50 i.e., the thin cord of her bodice (to give her easier breathing)
51 as long as
52 testimony
53 assumes/takes on
54 ONorABle
55 good now = please
56 suitable, proper★

Cleopatra   And target.[57] Still he mends.[58]

But this is not the best. Look prithee, Charmian,

How this Herculean Roman does become   85

The carriage of his chafe.[59]

Antony   I'll leave you, lady.

Cleopatra Courteous lord, one word.

Sir, you and I must part, but that's not it.

Sir, you and I have loved, but there's not it.

That you know well, something it is I would.[60]   90

O my oblivion[61] is a very[62] Antony,

And I am all forgotten.

Antony   But that your royalty

Holds idleness your subject,[63] I should take you

For idleness itself.

Cleopatra   'Tis sweating labor

To bear such idleness so near the heart   95

As Cleopatra this.[64] But sir, forgive me,

Since my becomings[65] kill me, when they do not

Eye well to you. Your honor calls you hence,

Therefore be deaf to my unpitied folly,

And all the gods go with you. Upon your sword   100

---

57 shield
58 still he mends = he goes on improving
59 become the carriage of his chafe = turns into/comes to be the vehicle/
    actor-out of his passion/fury
60 wish, want (she thus indicates an inability, at the moment, to recall exactly
    what "it" is)
61 forgetfulness
62 a very = is just like/a true★
63 holds idleness your subject = maintains★ sovereignty over idleness
64 bears this
65 graces, graceful actions

Sit laurel victory, and smooth[66] success
Be strewed before your feet!

Antony   Let us[67] go. Come.
Our separation so abides and flies[68]
That thou, residing here, goes yet with me,
105   And I, hence fleeting,[69] here remain with thee.
Away!

EXEUNT

66 serene, untroubled
67 i.e., first person singular (the royal "we"), Antony alone
68 abides and flies = remains★ and at the same time travels swiftly away
69 passing swiftly off

SCENE 4

Rome, Octavius Caesar's house

ENTER OCTAVIUS CAESAR, READING A LETTER,
LEPIDUS, AND THEIR ATTENDANTS

Caesar You may see, Lepidus, and henceforth know,[1]
It is not Caesar's natural vice,[2] to hate
Our great competitor.[3] From Alexandria
This is the news. He fishes, drinks, and wastes
The lamps of night in revel;[4] is not more manlike   5
Than Cleopatra, nor the queen of Ptolemy[5]
More womanly than he; hardly gave audience, or
Vouchsafed[6] to think he had partners. You shall find there
A man who is the abstract[7] of all faults
That all men follow.[8]

Lepidus   I must[9] not think there are   10
Evils enow[10] to darken all his goodness.
His faults in him seem as the spots[11] of heaven,
More fiery by[12] night's blackness, hereditary
Rather than purchased[13] – what he cannot change,

1 you MAY see LEpiDUS and HENCEforth KNOW
2 immorality, depravity
3 (1) competitor, *or* (2) associate, partner★
4 merrymaking
5 queen of Ptolemy = Cleopatra: Caesar had forced her to marry her younger
  brother of that name
6 condescended★
7 epitome, compendium, ideal
8 pursue, adhere to
9 can
10 enough (iNOW)
11 stars ("luminous points")
12 alongside, because of
13 acquired

15   Than[14] what he chooses.

    Caesar You are too indulgent. Let us grant it is not

    Amiss[15] to tumble[16] on the bed of Ptolemy,

    To give a kingdom for a mirth,[17] to sit

    And keep the turn of tippling[18] with a slave,

20   To reel[19] the streets at noon, and stand the buffet[20]

    With knaves that smell of sweat. Say this becomes him

    (As his composure[21] must be rare indeed

    Whom these things cannot blemish), yet must Antony

    No way excuse his soils,[22] when we[23] do bear

25   So great weight in[24] his lightness. If he filled

    His vacancy[25] with his voluptuousness,

    Full surfeits,[26] and the dryness of his bones,[27]

    Call on[28] him for't. But to confound such time

    That drums him[29] from his sport, and[30] speaks as loud

30   As his own state, and ours, 'tis[31] to be chid

---

14 rather than
15 wrong★
16 wallow
17 diversion, sport, merriment
18 keep the turn of tippling = take turns drinking
19 rush/prance/stagger around
20 stand the buffet = be exposed to the pushing/shoving/blows
21 temperament/constitution
22 stains
23 i.e., the other two triumvirs, Caesar and Lepidus
24 because of
25 free time, leisure
26 full surfeits = total excesses
27 dryness of his bones = (?) laziness? dullness?
28 call on = confront, challenge, accuse
29 that drums him = as calls him away from
30 and which
31 this needs

As we rate[32] boys, who being mature in knowledge
Pawn[33] their experience to their present pleasure,
And so rebel to judgment.[34]

ENTER A MESSENGER

Lepidus Here's more news.

Messenger Thy biddings have been done, and every hour,   35
Most noble Caesar, shalt thou have report
How 'tis abroad.[35] Pompey is strong at sea,
And it appears he is beloved of those
That only have feared[36] Caesar. To the ports
The discontents[37] repair, and men's reports   40
Give him[38] much wronged.

Caesar   I should have known no less.
It hath been taught us from the primal[39] state
That he which is[40] was wished[41] until he were,[42]
And the ebbed man,[43] ne'er loved till ne'er worth love,
Comes deared[44] by being lacked. This common body,[45]   45
Like to a vagabond flag[46] upon the stream,

32 scold, reprove
33 risk, wager
34 rebel to judgment = challenge good sense/wisdom/reason
35 spreading around the world (outside the city of Rome)
36 i.e., who have not loved/supported
37 the discontented
38 give him = make him out to be
39 original, earliest, most primitive
40 is in power
41 desired, favored
42 was in power
43 ebbed man = the man who was been left behind
44 comes deared = becomes wanted/loved
45 common body = the general public
46 vagabond flag = wandering/straying water-flag (a kind of iris)

Goes to, and back, lackeying[47] the varying tide,
To rot[48] itself with motion.

Messenger   Caesar, I bring thee word,
Menecrates and Menas,[49] famous pirates,
50   Make the sea serve them, which they ear[50] and wound
With keels of every kind. Many hot inroads
They make in Italy; the borders maritime
Lack blood[51] to think on't, and flush[52] youth revolt.
No vessel can peep forth, but 'tis as soon
55   Taken[53] as seen, for Pompey's name strikes more
Than could[54] his war resisted.[55]

Caesar   Antony,
Leave thy lascivious wassails.[56] When thou once
Wast beaten from Modena,[57] where thou slew'st
Hirtius and Pansa,[58] consuls, at thy heel
60   Did famine follow, whom thou fought'st against,
Though daintily[59] brought up, with patience more
Than savages could suffer. Thou didst drink
The stale[60] of horses, and the gilded[61] puddle

47 fawning upon
48 to rot = and rots
49 meNECKreTEEZ and MAYnis
50 plough
51 (1) vigor, spirit, *or* (2) manpower
52 lively, vigorous
53 captured
54 those who could have
55 (1) withstood, opposed, prevented, (2) fought against
56 lascivious wassails = lewd/voluptuous/luxurious festivities/drinking bouts
57 Italian city that he was besieging (moDANEah)
58 associates of Julius Caesar (HIRteeus)
59 elegantly, richly
60 urine
61 covered over with shiny, yellow-colored scum

Which beasts would cough at.[62] Thy palate[63] then did deign[64]
The roughest[65] berry on the rudest[66] hedge.   65
Yea, like the stag, when snow the pasture sheets,[67]
The barks of trees thou browsed'st.[68] On the Alps
It is reported thou didst eat strange flesh,
Which some did die to look on. And all this
(It wounds thine honor that I speak it now)   70
Was borne so like a soldier, that thy cheek
So much as lanked[69] not.

Lepidus   'Tis pity[70] of him.

Caesar   Let his shames quickly
Drive him to Rome. 'Tis time we twain
Did show ourselves i' the field, and to that end   75
Assemble we immediate[71] council. Pompey
Thrives in our idleness.

Lepidus   Tomorrow Caesar,
I shall be furnished[72] to inform you rightly
Both what by sea and land I can be able
To front[73] this present time.

Caesar   Till which encounter,[74]   80

62 cough at = cough out, spit up
63 taste, appetite
64 consider edible
65 bristly, harsh, disagreeable
66 most rugged/barbarous/coarse/wild
67 (verb) covers
68 fed on
69 shrank
70 regrettable
71 an immediate
72 equipped, readied, prepared
73 confront
74 meeting

It is[75] my business too. Farewell.

Lepidus Farewell, my lord. What you shall know meantime
Of stirs abroad, I shall beseech you sir
To let me be partaker.[76]

Caesar   Doubt not sir,
85   I knew it for my bond.[77]

EXEUNT

75 it is = that will be
76 a partaker
77 duty, obligation

SCENE 5

Alexandria, Cleopatra's palace

ENTER CLEOPATRA, CHARMIAN, IRAS, AND MARDIAN

Cleopatra Charmian!

Charmian Madam?

Cleopatra (*yawning*) Ha, ha.
  Give me to drink mandragora.[1]

Charmian Why, madam?   5

Cleopatra That I might sleep out this great gap of time
  My Antony is away.

Charmian   You think of him too much.

Cleopatra O 'tis[2] treason.

Charmian   Madam, I trust not so.

Cleopatra Thou, eunuch[3] Mardian!

Mardian   What's your Highness'
  pleasure?

Cleopatra Not now to hear thee sing. I take no pleasure   10
  In aught[4] an eunuch has. 'Tis well for thee
  That, being unseminared,[5] thy freer thoughts
  May not fly forth of Egypt.[6] Hast thou affections?[7]

Mardian Yes gracious madam.

Cleopatra Indeed?   15

1 mandrake, an herbal narcotic (manDRAgaruh)
2 that is
3 castrated man, generally, but here specifically a castrato with a boy's high vocal
  range (YOOnik)
4 anything
5 castrated
6 forth of Egypt = away from me
7 emotions, passions

Mardian   Not in deed madam, for I can do nothing

But what indeed is honest[8] to be done.

Yet have I fierce affections, and think

What Venus did with Mars.

Cleopatra   O Charmian,

20   Where think'st thou he is now? Stands he, or sits he?

Or does he walk? Or is he on his horse?

O happy horse, to bear the weight of Antony!

Do bravely, horse, for wot'st thou[9] whom thou movest,[10]

The demi-Atlas[11] of this earth, the arm

25   And burgonet[12] of men? He's speaking now,

Or murmuring, "Where's my serpent of old Nile?"

(For so he calls me). Now I feed myself

With most delicious poison. Think[13] on me

That am with Phoebus'[14] amorous pinches black,

30   And wrinkled deep in time.[15] Broad-fronted Caesar,[16]

When thou wast here above the ground, I was

A morsel[17] for a monarch. And great Pompey

Would stand and make his eyes grow in my brow,[18]

There would he anchor his aspect,[19] and die

8 chaste★

9 wot'st thou = do you know

10 put in motion, carry about

11 Titan, who held up the sky

12 arm and burgonet = chain-mail armor and steel battle helmet
   (BURRguNET)

13 addressing Antony

14 the sun god,★ who tans Cleopatra's already dark skin

15 i.e., growing older and more wrinkled

16 broad-fronted Caesar = Julius Caesar, with your broad forehead

17 choice dish (i.e., she was younger and more beautiful)

18 i.e., he would stare at her face

19 anchor his aspect = fix his look/gaze/sight

With[20] looking on[21] his life.   35

ENTER ALEXAS, FROM ANTONY

Alexas   Sovereign of Egypt, hail!

Cleopatra How much unlike art thou[22] Mark Antony!
     Yet coming from him, that great med'cine[23] hath
     With his tinct[24] gilded thee.
     How goes it with my brave Mark Antony?   40

Alexas   Last thing he did, dear Queen,
     He kissed (the last of many doubled kisses)
     This orient[25] pearl. His speech sticks[26] in my heart.

Cleopatra Mine ear must pluck it thence.

Alexas   "Good friend,"
     quoth he,
     "Say, the firm[27] Roman to great Egypt sends   45
     This treasure of[28] an oyster. At whose foot,
     To mend the petty[29] present, I will piece[30]
     Her opulent throne with kingdoms. All the east,
     Say thou, shall call her mistress." So he nodded,
     And soberly[31] did mount an arm-gaunt[32] steed,   50

20 from
21 at
22 you to
23 cure, remedy (i.e., Antony)
24 coloring, hue
25 brilliant, precious
26 is fixed, remains permanently
27 constant, steady
28 from
29 insignificant, trivial★
30 complete, make whole, repair
31 somberly, gravely
32 (?) arm-gaunt = armored (most armorial English words being from the

Who neighed so high,[33] that what I would have spoke
Was beastly dumbed[34] by him.

Cleopatra What, was he sad, or merry?

Alexas   Like to the time o' the year between the extremes

55   Of hot and cold, he was nor[35] sad nor merry.

Cleopatra O well–divided disposition![36] Note him,
Note him good Charmian, 'tis the man. But[37] note him.
He was not sad, for he would[38] shine on those
That make[39] their looks by his. He was not merry,

60   Which seemed to tell them his remembrance lay
In Egypt with his joy; but between both.
O heavenly mingle! Be'st thou sad or merry,
The violence[40] of either thee[41] becomes,
So does it no man else. Met'st thou my posts?

65 *Alexas*   Ay madam, twenty several messengers.
Why do you send so thick?[42]

Cleopatra   Who's born that day
When I forget to send to Antony,
Shall die a beggar. Ink and paper, Charmian.
Welcome, my good Alexas. Did I, Charmian,
Ever love Caesar so?

French, this may mean leather gauntlets for the upper part of the horse's legs,
 to protect it from the swords and spears of unmounted enemies)
33 strongly, loudly
34 beastly dumbed = abominably / offensively / exceedingly silenced
35 neither
36 (1) arrangement, managing, control, (2) character, frame of mind
37 just
38 wished to
39 frame, fashion
40 force, strength, intensity
41 Antony
42 (adverb) excessively, frequently

Charmian　　　　　　O that brave Caesar!　　　　　　　　70

Cleopatra　Be choked with such another emphasis!
　　Say, the brave Antony.

Charmian　　　　　　The valiant Caesar!

Cleopatra　By Isis, I will give thee bloody teeth,
　　If thou with Caesar paragon[43] again
　　My man of men.

Charmian　　　　　By your most gracious pardon,　　　75
　　I sing but after[44] you.

Cleopatra　　　　　　My salad days,
　　When I was green in judgment. Cold in blood,
　　To say as I said then! But come, away,
　　Get me ink and paper.
　　He shall have every day a several[45] greeting,　　　80
　　Or I'll unpeople Egypt.

EXEUNT

---

43 compare
44 following
45 different, separate

Act 2

SCENE I

Messina, Pompey's house

ENTER POMPEY, MENECRATES, AND MENAS,
IN WARLIKE MANNER

Pompey   If the great gods be just, they shall assist
The deeds of justest men.

Menecrates   Know, worthy Pompey,
That what they do delay, they not deny.

Pompey   Whiles we are suitors to their throne, decays
The thing we sue for.

5   *Menecrates*   We, ignorant of ourselves,
Beg often our own harms, which the wise powers
Deny us for our good. So find we profit
By losing of our prayers.

Pompey   I shall do well.
The people love me, and the sea is mine.

10   My powers are crescent,[1] and my auguring[2] hope

1 growing, waxing
2 prophetic

38

Says it will come to the full. Mark Antony
In Egypt sits at dinner, and will make
No wars without doors.[3] Caesar gets money where
He loses hearts. Lepidus flatters both,
Of both is flattered. But he neither loves,   15
Nor either[4] cares for him.

Menas   Caesar and Lepidus
Are in the field. A mighty strength they carry.

Pompey Where have you this? 'tis false.

Menas   From Silvius, sir.

Pompey He dreams. I know they are in Rome together,
Looking for[5] Antony. But all the charms of love,   20
Salt[6] Cleopatra, soften thy waned[7] lip!
Let witchcraft join with beauty, lust with both!
Tie up the libertine in a field of feasts,
Keep his brain fuming. Epicurean[8] cooks
Sharpen with cloyless[9] sauce his appetite,   25
That sleep and feeding may prorogue[10] his honor
Even till a Lethe'd[11] dullness!

ENTER VARRIUS

---

3 without doors = (1) away from home, *or* (2) in his state of excessive eating
  and drinking
4 nor either = and neither
5 looking for = expecting, anticipating
6 lecherous
7 diminished ("withering")
8 sensual, gluttonous
9 never cloying/surfeiting/satiating★
10 delay, postpone
11 Lethe: river in Hades, one sip of which produced forgetting of the past
  (LEEthee)★

39

         How now, Varrius.

Varrius This is most certain that I shall deliver.[12]

  Mark Antony is every hour in Rome

30 Expected. Since he went from Egypt 'tis

  A space for farther travel.[13]

  Pompey   I could have given less matter[14]

  A better ear. Menas, I did not think

  This amorous surfeiter would have donned his helm

  For such a petty war. His soldiership

35 Is twice[15] the other twain. But let us rear[16]

  The higher our opinion, that our stirring

  Can from the lap of Egypt's widow pluck

  The ne'er-lust-wearied Antony.

  Menas   I cannot hope[17]

  Caesar and Antony shall well greet together.

40 His wife that's dead did trespasses[18] to Caesar,

  His brother warred upon him, although I think

  Not moved by Antony.

  Pompey   I know not, Menas,

  How lesser enmities[19] may give way to[20] greater.

  Were't not that we stand up[21] against them all,

---

12 report, say

13 a space for farther travel = a time sufficient for even a longer trip

14 substance ("fewer words")

15 double that of the other

16 raise, lift

17 expect

18 wrongs

19 feelings of hatred/hostility

20 give way to = retreat/dissolve/disappear in the face of (i.e., how Caesar and Antony could put aside their differences in the face of Pompey's greater threat)

21 stand up = take a stand

'Twere pregnant[22] they should square[23] between themselves,   45
For they have entertainèd[24] cause enough
To draw their swords. But how the fear of us
May cement their divisions[25] and bind up
The petty difference, we yet not know.
Be't as our gods will have't! It only stands[26]   50
Our lives upon to use our strongest hands.
Come Menas.

EXEUNT

22 plain
23 quarrel★
24 provided
25 disagreements, discords★
26 depends

SCENE 2
Rome, Lepidus' house

ENTER ENOBARBUS AND LEPIDUS

Lepidus   Good Enobarbus, 'tis a worthy deed,
    And shall become you well, to entreat your captain
    To soft and gentle[1] speech.

Enobarbus   I shall entreat him
    To answer like himself. If Caesar move[2] him,
5   Let Antony look over[3] Caesar's head
    And speak as loud as Mars. By Jupiter,
    Were I the wearer of Antonius' beard,
    I would not shave't today.[4]

Lepidus   'Tis not a time
    For private stomaching.[5]

Enobarbus   Every time
10   Serves for the matter that is then born in't.

Lepidus   But small to greater matters must give way.

Enobarbus Not if the small come first.

Lepidus   Your speech is passion.
    But pray you, stir no embers up. Here comes
    The noble Antony.

ENTER ANTONY AND VENTIDIUS

1 well-born, gentlemanly★
2 disturb, agitate, provoke
3 (i.e., Antony being a much taller man, could readily "look over" Caesar's head)
4 (?) *either* (1) change anything, regardless, *or* (2) concede anything for Caesar's sake
5 (1) stubbornness, irritations, anger, (2) passions, feelings★

Enobarbus   And yonder, Caesar.

ENTER OCTAVIUS CAESAR, MAECENAS, AND AGRIPPA

Antony   If we compose[6] well here, to Parthia.   15
  Hark, Ventidius.[7]
Caesar   (*to Maecenas*) I do not know,
  Maecenas,[8] ask Agrippa.
Lepidus   Noble friends,
  That which combined us was most great, and let not
  A leaner[9] action rend us.[10] What's amiss,   20
  May it be gently heard. When we debate
  Our trivial difference loud, we do commit
  Murder in healing wounds. Then noble partners,
  The rather,[11] for I earnestly beseech,
  Touch you the sourest points with sweetest terms,   25
  Nor curstness[12] grow to the matter.
Antony   'Tis spoken well.
  Were we before[13] our armies, and to fight,
  I should do thus.[14]

FLOURISH

Caesar   Welcome to Rome.
Antony   Thank you.

6 settle quarrels★
7 hark, Ventidius = listen,★ venTIdeeUS
8 mySEEnus
9 slighter, lesser
10 rend us = tear us apart
11 the rather = instead
12 vexation
13 in front of
14 do thus = proceed in exactly that way

Caesar Sit.

30 *Antony* Sit sir.

Caesar Nay then.

CAESAR AND ANTONY SEAT THEMSELVES

Antony I learn, you take things ill which are not so,
        Or being,[15] concern you not.

Caesar   I must[16] be laughed at,
        If, or[17] for nothing or a little, I

35   Should say myself offended, and with you
        Chiefly i' the world. More laughed at, that I should
        Once name you derogately,[18] when to sound your name
        It not concerned me.

Antony   My being in Egypt, Caesar,
        What was't to you?

40 *Caesar* No more than my residing here at Rome
        Might be to you in Egypt. Yet if you there
        Did practice on[19] my state, your being in Egypt
        Might be my question.[20]

Antony   How intend you, "practiced"?

Caesar You may be pleased to catch at mine intent

45   By what did here befall[21] me. Your wife and brother
        Made wars upon me, and their contestation[22]

---

15 being so
16 ought to/should be
17 either
18 derogatorily, disparagingly
19 practice on = operate/plan/scheme against
20 point to be discussed*
21 happen/occur to
22 struggle, conflict

Was theme for you,[23] you were the word of war.[24]

Antony You do mistake your business,[25] my brother never

 Did urge me in his act. I did inquire[26] it,

 And have my learning from some true reports   50

 That[27] drew their swords with you. Did he not rather

 Discredit my authority with[28] yours,

 And make the wars alike against my stomach,

 Having alike[29] your cause?[30] Of this my letters

 Before did satisfy you. If you'll patch[31] a quarrel,   55

 As matter whole you have[32] to make it with,

 It must not be with this.[33]

Caesar   You praise yourself

 By laying defects of judgment to me – but

 You patched up your excuses.

Antony   Not so, not so.

 I know you could not lack (I am certain on't)[34]   60

 Very necessity of this thought,[35] that I,

 Your partner in the cause 'gainst which he fought,

 Could not with graceful[36] eyes attend[37] those wars

23 theme for you = based upon you, had you as its cause
24 word of war = what the war was said to be about
25 your business = what you're concerned about
26 investigate
27 of those who
28 together with
29 having alike = since I shared
30 goals, purposes
31 mend, make up
32 as matter whole you have = since you have sound/good substance
33 i.e., which is *not* sound
34 of it
35 very necessity of this thought = being truly obliged to realize
36 friendly, favorable
37 regard, look

Which fronted[38] mine own peace. As for my wife,
65   I would you had her spirit in such another.
    The third o' the world is yours, which with a snaffle[39]
    You may pace[40] easy, but not such a wife.

Enobarbus Would we had all such wives, that the men might go
    to wars with the women!

Antony   So much uncurbable, her garboils, Caesar,
70   Made out of her impatience (which not wanted[41]
    Shrewdness of policy too), I grieving grant
    Did you too much disquiet. For that you must
    But say I could not help it.

Caesar   I wrote to you
    When rioting in Alexandria you
75   Did pocket up my letters, and with taunts
    Did gibe my missive[42] out of audience.

Antony   Sir,
    He fell upon me ere admitted,[43] then.
    Three kings I had newly feasted, and did want
    Of what I was i' the morning.[44] But next day
80   I told him of myself,[45] which was as much
    As to have asked him pardon. Let this fellow
    Be nothing of our strife. If we contend,
    Out of our question wipe him.

---

38 directly opposed
39 light hand (snaffle = a bridle bit: i.e., using a lighter hand to control a horse)
40 train
41 not wanted = did not lack★
42 gibe my missive = jeered my messenger
43 received, permitted
44 i.e., he had a hangover
45 of myself = on my own initiative

Caesar   You have broken

The article[46] of your oath, which you shall never

Have tongue to charge[47] me with.

Lepidus   Soft,[48] Caesar!

Antony   No,   85

Lepidus, let him speak.

The honor is sacred which he talks on now,

Supposing that I lacked it. But on,[49] Caesar,

The article of my oath.

Caesar   To lend me arms[50] and aid when I required them,   90

The which you both denied.

Antony   Neglected, rather.

And then when poisoned[51] hours had bound me up[52]

From mine own knowledge. As nearly as I may,

I'll play the penitent to you. But mine honesty

Shall not make poor my greatness,[53] nor my power   95

Work without it.[54] Truth is, that Fulvia,

To have me out of Egypt, made wars here,

For which myself, the ignorant motive, do

So far ask pardon as befits mine honor

To stoop in such a case.

Lepidus   'Tis noble spoken.   100

Maecenas If it might please you, to enforce no further

46 conditions, terms
47 have tongue to charge = be able to accuse
48 retrain yourself, be calm
49 go on, continue
50 soldiers
51 potions, malignant drugs
52 bound me up = enclosed me away
53 make poor my greatness = deprecate my high rank
54 my high rank

The griefs[55] between ye. To forget them quite[56]
Were to remember that the present need
Speaks to atone[57] you.

Lepidus   Worthily spoken, Maecenas.

105 *Enobarbus* Or if you borrow one another's love for the instant,
you may when you hear no more words of Pompey return it
again. You shall have time to wrangle in when you have
nothing else to do.

Antony   Thou art a soldier only;[58] speak no more.

110 *Enobarbus* That truth should be silent I had almost forgot.

Antony   You wrong this presence,[59] therefore speak no more.

Enobarbus Go to,[60] then. Your considerate stone.[61]

Caesar   I do not much dislike the matter, but
The manner of his[62] speech. For't[63] cannot be

115 We shall remain in friendship, our conditions[64]
So differing in their acts. Yet if I knew
What hoop[65] should hold us stanch,[66] from edge to edge
O' the world I would pursue it.

Agrippa   Give me leave, Caesar.

Caesar   Speak, Agrippa.

120 *Agrippa*   Thou hast a sister by the mother's side,

55 wrongs, offenses, grievances
56 completely, altogether★
57 reconcile, unite
58 just
59 honorable company
60 go to = all right, come on★
61 considerate stone = I will remain a thinking man but silent as a stone
62 Antony's
63 because of that, it
64 natures
65 circular fastener, wood or metal (as in "barrel hoop")
66 staunch, firm

    Admired Octavia. Great Mark Antony
    Is now a widower.

Caesar   Say not so, Agrippa.
    If Cleopatra heard you, your reproof
    Were well deserved of [67] rashness.

Antony   I am not married, Caesar. Let me hear   125
    Agrippa further speak.

Agrippa   To hold you in perpetual amity,
    To make you brothers, and to knit your hearts
    With an unslipping knot, take Antony
    Octavia to his wife, whose beauty claims   130
    No worse a husband than the best of men,
    Whose virtue and whose general graces speak
    That which none else can utter. By this marriage,
    All little jealousies which now seem great,
    And all great fears, which now import their dangers,   135
    Would then be nothing. Truths would be tales,
    Where now half tales be truths. Her love to both
    Would each to other, and all loves to both
    Draw after her. Pardon what I have spoke,
    For 'tis a studied [68] not a present thought,   140
    By duty ruminated. [69]

Antony   Will Caesar speak?

Caesar   Not till he hears how Antony is touched [70]
    With what is spoke already.

Antony   What power is in Agrippa,

---

67 for its
68 premeditated, carefully prepared★
69 considered, meditated
70 affected, moved★

If I would say "Agrippa, be it so,"
To make this good?[71]

145 *Caesar*   The power of Caesar, and
His power unto Octavia.

Antony   May I never
To this good purpose, that so fairly shows,[72]
Dream of impediment! Let me have thy hand,
Further[73] this act of grace.[74] And from this hour
150 The heart of brothers govern in our loves
And sway our great designs.

Caesar   There is my hand.
A sister I bequeath[75] you, whom no brother
Did ever love so dearly. Let her live
To join our kingdoms, and our hearts, and never
Fly off[76] our loves again!

155 *Lepidus*   Happily, amen!

Antony I did not think to draw my sword 'gainst Pompey,
For he hath laid strange courtesies and great
Of late upon me. I must thank him only,[77]
Lest my remembrance[78] suffer ill report.
At heel of[79] that, defy[80] him.

160 *Lepidus*   Time calls upon's.

---

71 make this good = carry this out, fulfill/perform this
72 so fairly shows = shows itself so suitably/well
73 in order to advance/move forward
74 goodwill, favor★
75 give, entrust
76 fly off = break away
77 thank him only = simply (and no more than that) thank him
78 memory
79 at heel of = and right after
80 challenge (to combat)

Of us must Pompey presently be sought,

Or else he seeks out us.

Antony   Where lies he?

Caesar   About the mount Misena.[81]

Antony   What is his strength by

land?

Caesar   Great and increasing. But by sea

He is an absolute master.

Antony   So is the fame.[82]   165

Would we had spoke together![83] Haste we for[84] it:

Yet ere we put ourselves in arms, dispatch[85] we

The business we have talked of.

Caesar   With most gladness,

And do invite you to my sister's view,[86]

Whither straight I'll lead you.

Antony   Let us, Lepidus,   170

Not lack your company.

Lepidus   Noble Antony,

Not sickness should detain me!

FLOURISH

EXEUNT CAESAR, ANTONY, AND LEPIDUS

Maecenas   Welcome from Egypt, sir.

Enobarbus   Half the heart of Caesar, worthy Maecenas! My

81 SW Italy★
82 so is the fame = that is the general talk
83 spoke together = consulted each other (i.e., Antony and Caesar)
84 toward
85 dispose of, finish★
86 inspection, examination (mutual? or, more likely, Antony's inspection of
    her?)

175   honorable friend, Agrippa!

Agrippa   Good Enobarbus!

Maecenas   We have cause to be glad that matters are so well
        digested.[87] You stayed well by't[88] in Egypt.

Enobarbus   Ay sir, we did sleep day out of countenance,[89] and
180   made the night light with drinking.

Maecenas   Eight wild boars roasted whole at a breakfast, and but
        twelve persons there. Is this true?

Enobarbus   This was but as a fly by[90] an eagle. We had much
        more monstrous matter of feast, which worthily deserved
185   noting.

Maecenas   She's a most triumphant lady, if report be square[91] to
        her.

Enobarbus   When she first met Mark Antony, she pursed up[92] his
        heart, upon the river of Cydnus.[93]

190 *Agrippa*   There she appeared indeed. Or my reporter devised[94]
        well for her.

Enobarbus   I will tell you.

        The barge she sat in, like a burnished[95] throne
        Burned[96] on the water. The poop[97] was beaten gold,
195   Purple the sails, and so perfumed that
        The winds were love-sick with them. The oars were silver,

87 ordered
88 stayed well by't = rested comfortably
89 day out of countenance = more than daylight could believe
90 in comparison to
91 fair
92 pursed up = took possession of
93 SIDnus, SE Asia Minor
94 invented
95 polished, shining
96 gleamed, blazed with light
97 stern

Which to the tune of flutes kept stroke, and made

The water which they beat to follow faster,

As[98] amorous of their strokes. For her own person,

It beggared[99] all description, she did lie   200

In her pavilion, cloth-of-gold of tissue,[100]

O'er-picturing[101] that Venus where we see

The fancy outwork[102] nature. On each side her

Stood pretty dimpled boys, like smiling Cupids,

With divers-colored[103] fans, whose wind[104] did seem   205

To glow the delicate cheeks which they did cool,

And what they undid did.[105]

Agrippa   O rare[106] for Antony!

Enobarbus Her gentlewomen, like the Nereides,[107]

So many mermaids, tended her i' th' eyes,[108]

And made their bends[109] adornings. At the helm   210

A seeming mermaid steers. The silken tackle[110]

Swell with the touches of those flower-soft hands,

That yarely frame[111] the office. From the barge

A strange invisible perfume hits the sense

---

 98 as if

 99 outdid, surpassed

100 stately tent of rich cloth interwoven with gold

101 o'er-picturing = exaggerating, surpassing

102 fancy outwork (verb) = imagination★ surpass

103 different colored

104 i.e., the air stirred by the boys' fans

105 i.e., the heat of the air, which they took away, was replaced by Cleopatra's "glow"

106 wonderful, exceptional★

107 sea maidens (NEARiDEEZ)

108 i' th' eyes = openly, visibly

109 changes in posture ("bendings")

110 rigging, gear (then perceived as a plural noun)

111 yarely frame = nimbly★ perform

215   Of the adjacent wharfs.[112] The city cast[113]
       Her people out upon her. And Antony,
       Enthroned i' the market-place, did sit alone,
       Whistling to the air, which, but for vacancy,[114]
       Had gone to gaze on Cleopatra too,
       And made a gap in nature.

220 *Agrippa*   Rare Egyptian!

    Enobarbus Upon her landing, Antony sent to her,
       Invited her to supper. She replied,
       It should be better, he became her guest,
       Which she entreated. Our courteous Antony,

225   Whom ne'er the word of "No" woman heard speak,
       Being barbered[115] ten times o'er, goes to the feast,
       And for his ordinary[116] pays his heart
       For what his eyes eat only.

    Agrippa   Royal wench!
       She made great Caesar lay his sword to bed.
       He ploughed her, and she cropped.[117]

230 *Enobarbus*   I saw her once
       Hop forty paces through the public street,
       And having lost her breath, she spoke, and panted,
       That[118] she did make defect[119] perfection,
       And, breathless,[120] power breathe forth.

112 banks
113 threw forth
114 but for vacancy = except that it would then have created a vacuum
115 groomed
116 meal
117 reaped, had a crop ("became pregnant and bore a son")
118 so that
119 a flaw into a (DEEfect)
120 although breathless

Maecenas   Now Antony must leave her utterly.   235

Enobarbus   Never he will not.

   Age cannot wither her, nor custom stale[121]

   Her infinite variety. Other women cloy

   The appetites they feed, but she makes hungry

   Where most she satisfies. For vilest things   240

   Become themselves[122] in her, that the holy priests

   Bless her when she is riggish.[123]

Mecaenas   If beauty, wisdom, modesty, can settle

   The heart of Antony, Octavia is

   A blessèd lottery[124] to him.

Agrippa   Let us go.   245

   Good Enobarbus, make yourself my guest

   Whilst you abide here.

Enobarbus   Humbly sir, I thank you.

EXEUNT

121 custom stale = habit diminish, make stale
122 become themselves = make themselves becoming/proper/suitable
123 wanton, licentious
124 luck, fortune, prize

SCENE 3

Rome, Caesar's house

ENTER ANTONY, CAESAR, WITH OCTAVIA
BETWEEN THEM, AND ATTENDANTS

Antony   The world and my great office will sometimes
      Divide me from your bosom.

Octavia   All which time
      Before the gods my knee shall bow my prayers
      To them for you.

Antony   (*to Caesar*) Good night sir. My Octavia,
5   Read not my blemishes in the world's report.
      I have not kept my square,[1] but that to come
      Shall all be done by the rule. Good night, dear lady.
      Good night, sir.

Caesar   Good night.

EXEUNT CAESAR AND OCTAVIA

ENTER SOOTHSAYER

10   *Antony*   Now sirrah.[2] You do wish yourself in Egypt?

Soothsayer Would I had never come from thence, nor you
      thither!

Antony   If you can, your reason?

Soothsayer   I see it in
      My motion,[3] have it not in my tongue. But yet
      Hie[4] you to Egypt again.

Antony   Say to me,

---

1 kept my square = followed a straight line (square: a carpenter's rule)
2 form of address to lower-ranking adults and all children
3 emotions, inner self
4 hurry★

Whose fortunes shall rise higher, Caesar's or mine?   15
Soothsayer Caesar's.
    Therefore, O Antony, stay not by his side.
    Thy daemon,[5] that[6] thy spirit which keeps[7] thee, is
    Noble, courageous high, unmatchable,
    Where Caesar's is not. But near him, thy angel   20
    Becomes a fear, as[8] being o'erpowered. Therefore
    Make space enough between you.
Antony   Speak this no more.
Soothsayer To none but thee no more, but when to thee,
    If thou dost play with him at any game,
    Thou art sure to lose. And of that natural luck,   25
    He beats thee 'gainst the odds. Thy luster thickens,[9]
    When he shines by. I say again, thy spirit
    Is all afraid to govern thee near him.
    But he away,[10] 'tis noble.
Antony   Get thee gone.
    Say to Ventidius I would speak with him.   30

                    EXIT SOOTHSAYER

He shall[11] to Parthia. Be it art or hap,[12]
He[13] hath spoken true. The very dice obey him,[14]
And in our sports my better cunning faints

5 attendant, ministering spirit (i.e., *not* a demon)
6 that is
7 takes care of
8 as if
9 clouds over
10 Folio: alway; all editors emend
11 he shall = Ventidius must go
12 art or hap = skill or luck
13 the Soothsayer
14 Caesar

Under his chance.[15] If we draw lots, he speeds,[16]
35   His cocks do win the battle still[17] of mine,
When it is all to nought,[18] and his quails ever
Beat mine, inhooped,[19] at odds.[20] I will to Egypt.
And though I make this marriage for my peace,
I' the east my pleasure lies.

ENTER VENTIDIUS

           O come, Ventidius,
40   You must to Parthia, your commission's ready.
Follow me, and receive't.

EXEUNT

15 luck, fortune★
16 prospers, succeeds
17 always
18 it is all to nought = the odds are 100% to 0%
19 put in a fighting ring
20 at odds = against odds very much in Antony's favor

SCENE 4
Rome, a street

ENTER LEPIDUS, MAECENAS, AND AGRIPPA

Lepidus   Trouble yourselves no further. Pray you, hasten
　　Your generals after.
Agrippa　　　　　　　　Sir, Mark Antony
　　Will e'en but kiss Octavia, and we'll follow.
Lepidus   Till I shall see you in your soldier's dress,
　　Which will become you both, farewell.
Maecenas　　　　　　　　　　　We shall,　　　　　　5
　　As I conceive[1] the journey, be at the Mount[2]
　　Before you, Lepidus.
Lepidus　　　　　　Your way[3] is shorter,
　　My purposes do draw me much about.
　　You'll win two days upon me.
Maecenas and Agrippa　　　　Sir, good success!
Lepidus   Farewell.　　　　　　　　　　　　　　10

EXEUNT

1 consider, see
2 Mount Misena
3 road, path★

59

SCENE 5
Alexandria, Cleopatra's palace

ENTER CLEOPATRA, CHARMIAN, IRAS, AND ALEXAS

Cleopatra   Give me some music. Music, moody food
Of us that trade in love.
Attendants   The music, ho!

ENTER MARDIAN

Cleopatra   Let it alone, let's to billiards. Come Charmian.
Charmian   My arm is sore, best play with Mardian.
5 *Cleopatra*   As well a woman with an eunuch played
As with a woman. Come, you'll play with me sir?
Mardian   As well as I can, madam.
Cleopatra   And when good will is showed, though't come too
short,
The actor[1] may plead pardon. I'll none now,[2]
10 Give me mine angle,[3] we'll to the river. There,
My music playing far off, I will betray[4]
Tawny-finned fishes, my bended hook shall pierce
Their slimy jaws, and as I draw them up
I'll think them every one an Antony,
And say, "Ah, ha! you're caught."
15 *Charmian*   'Twas merry when
You wagered on your angling, when your diver[5]

---

1 person acting, doing
2 I'll none now = no, I don't want to play billiards, now
3 fishing gear
4 seduce, deceive
5 the person who dove and fetched for her (Antony?)

    Did hang[6] a salt-fish on his hook, which he
    With fervency[7] drew up.

Cleopatra   That time? O times[8]
    I laughed him out of patience,[9] and that night
    I laughed him into patience, and next morn,   20
    Ere the ninth hour, I drunk him to his bed.
    Then put my tires[10] and mantles on him, whilst
    I wore his sword Philippan.[11]

ENTER A MESSENGER

                         O, from Italy
    Ram[12] thou thy fruitful tidings in mine ears,
    That long time have been barren.

Messenger   Madam, madam –   25

Cleopatra   Antonius dead! If thou say so, villain,[13]
    Thou kill'st thy mistress. But well and free,
    If thou so yield[14] him. There is gold, and here
    My bluest veins to kiss – a hand that kings
    Have lipped, and trembled kissing.

Messenger   First, madam, he is well.   30

Cleopatra   Why, there's more gold. But sirrah, mark, we use[15]

---

  6 i.e., put it on the hook before he threw it into the water
  7 great feeling
  8 the times
  9 composure, calm★
 10 garments, dresses
 11 which Antony had worn at the Battle of Philippi, when he defeated Brutus
    and Cassius
 12 (verb) stuff, cram
 13 low-born rustic/scoundrel
 14 render, exhibit, deliver
 15 customarily★

To say the dead are well. Bring[16] it to that,
The gold I give thee will I melt and pour
Down thy ill-uttering throat.

Messenger   Good madam, hear me.

35 *Cleopatra* Well, go to, I will.
But there's no goodness in thy face, if Antony
Be free and healthful. So tart a favor[17]
To trumpet[18] such good tidings! If not well,
Thou shouldst come like a Fury[19] crowned with snakes,
Not like a formal man.[20]

40 *Messenger*   Will't please you hear me?

Cleopatra I have a mind to strike thee ere thou speak'st.
Yet if thou say Antony lives, is well,
Or friends with Caesar, or not captive to him,
I'll set thee in a shower of gold, and hail
Rich pearls upon thee.

Messenger   Madam, he's well.

45 *Cleopatra*   Well said.

Messenger And friends with Caesar.

Cleopatra   Thou'rt an honest[21] man.

Messenger Caesar and he are greater friends than ever.

Cleopatra Make thee[22] a fortune from me.

Messenger   But yet, madam –

Cleopatra I do not like "but yet," it does allay[23]

16 lead, conduct
17 tart a favor = sour a look/face
18 proclaim
19 avenging deity
20 like a formal man = looking like/having the shape/appearance of a man
21 honorable
22 make thee = you will have
23 debase, contaminate, annul

The good precedence, fie upon "but yet"! 50
"But yet" is as a jailor to bring forth
Some monstrous malefactor. Prithee, friend,
Pour out the pack[24] of matter to mine ear,
The good and bad together. He's friends with Caesar,
In state of health thou say'st, and thou say'st free. 55

Messenger Free madam, no. I made no such report,
He's bound unto Octavia.

Cleopatra   For what good turn?

Messenger For the best turn i' the bed.

Cleopatra   I am pale, Charmian.

Messenger Madam, he's married to Octavia.

Cleopatra The most infectious pestilence upon thee! 60

SHE STRIKES HIM DOWN

Messenger Good madam, patience.

Cleopatra   What say you?
(*striking him again*) Hence, horrible villain, or I'll spurn[25]
thine eyes
Like balls before me, I'll unhair thy head,
(*dragging him up and down*) Thou shalt be whipped with wire,
and stewed in brine,
Smarting in lingering pickle.[26]

Messenger   Gracious madam, 65
I that do bring the news, made not the match.

Cleopatra Say 'tis not so, a province I will give thee,

24 bundle, package
25 kick
26 smarting in lingering pickle = suffering in slow/protracted salty/acid
pickling solution

And make thy fortunes proud.[27] The blow thou hadst
Shall make thy peace, for moving me to rage,
70   And I will boot[28] thee with what gift beside
Thy modesty can beg.

Messenger   He's married, madam.

Cleopatra (*drawing a knife*) Rogue, thou hast lived too long.

Messenger   Nay,
then I'll run.
What mean you, madam? I have made no fault.

EXIT MESSENGER

Charmian Good madam, keep yourself within yourself,
75   The man is innocent.

Cleopatra Some innocents 'scape not the thunderbolt.
Melt Egypt into Nile! And kindly[29] creatures
Turn all to serpents! Call the slave again,
Though I am mad, I will not bite him. Call.

Charmian He is afeard to come.

80 *Cleopatra*   I will not hurt him.

EXIT CHARMIAN

These hands do lack nobility, that they strike
A meaner[30] than myself, since I myself
Have given myself the cause.

ENTER CHARMIAN AND MESSENGER

27 (1) satisfied, pleased, (2) exalted, gallant, splendid, luxuriant
28 enrich
29 proper, normal, natural
30 humbler, lower-ranking person

Come hither, sir.
Though it be honest, it is never good
To bring bad news. Give to a gracious message   85
An host of tongues, but let ill tidings tell
Themselves when they be felt.

Messenger   I have done my duty.

Cleopatra Is he married?
I cannot hate thee worser than I do,
If thou again say "Yes."

Messenger   He's married, madam.   90

Cleopatra The gods confound thee! Dost thou hold there still?

Messenger Should I lie, madam?

Cleopatra   O, I would thou didst!
So half my Egypt were submerged and made
A cistern[31] for scaled snakes! Go, get thee hence.[32]
Hadst thou Narcissus[33] in thy face, to me   95
Thou wouldst appear most ugly. He is married?

Messenger I crave[34] your Highness' pardon.

Cleopatra   He is married?

Messenger Take no offense that I would not[35] offend you.
To punish me for what you make me do
Seems much unequal.[36] He's married to Octavia.   100

Cleopatra O that his fault should make a knave of thee,
That art not[37] what thou'rt sure of! Get thee hence.

---

31 water tank
32 a SIStern FOR scaled SNAKES go GET thee HENCE
33 a singularly beautiful young man
34 beg, ask★
35 would not = do not wish to
36 unjust, unfair
37 not as wicked as

The merchandise which thou hast brought from Rome
Are all too dear for me. Lie they upon thy hand,[38]
105   And be undone[39] by 'em!

EXIT MESSENGER

Charmian Good your Highness, patience.
Cleopatra In praising Antony, I have dispraised Caesar.
Charmian Many times, madam.
Cleopatra   I am paid for't now.
    Lead me from hence,
110   I faint. O Iras, Charmian! 'Tis no matter.
    Go to the fellow, good Alexas, bid him
    Report the feature[40] of Octavia, her years,
    Her inclination,[41] let him not leave out
    The color of her hair. Bring me word quickly.

EXIT ALEXAS

115   Let him for ever go! Let him not! Charmian,
    Though he be painted one way like a Gorgon,[42]
    The other way's a Mars. (*to Mardian*) Bid you Alexas
    Bring me word how tall she is. Pity me, Charmian,
    But do not speak to me. Lead me to my chamber.

EXEUNT

---

38 lie they upon your hand = you keep them
39 ruined
40 (1) shape, proportions, (2) physical beauty
41 disposition, character
42 ghastly monsters, the sight of whom froze people; Medusa was a Gorgon

SCENE 6
Near Misenum

FLOURISH

ENTER POMPEY AND MENAS AT ONE DOOR, WITH DRUM AND
TRUMPET, AND AT ANOTHER CAESAR, ANTONY, LEPIDUS,
ENOBARBUS, MAECENAS, WITH SOLDIERS MARCHING

Pompey Your hostages I have, so have you mine.
And we shall talk before we fight.

Caesar   Most meet
That first we come to words, and therefore have we
Our written purposes before us sent,
Which if thou hast considered, let us know   5
If 'twill tie up thy discontented sword,
And carry back to Sicily much tall[1] youth
That else must perish here.

Pompey   To you all three,
The senators alone[2] of this great world,
Chief factors[3] for the gods, I do not know   10
Wherefore my father should revengers want,[4]
Having a son and friends, since Julius Caesar,
Who at Philippi the good Brutus ghosted,[5]
There saw you laboring for him. What was't
That moved pale[6] Cassius to conspire? And what   15
Made the all-honored, honest Roman, Brutus,

---

1 handsome, fine, bold, strong
2 senators alone = only rulers
3 agents
4 lack
5 i.e., Caesar, dead, there made a ghostly appearance to Brutus
6 timorous, dim, not intense

With the armed rest,[7] courtiers[8] of beauteous freedom,
To drench[9] the Capitol, but that they would
Have one man but[10] a man? And that is it
20   Hath made me rig[11] my navy (at whose burden
The angered ocean foams), with which I meant
To scourge the ingratitude that despiteful Rome
Cast on my noble father.

Caesar   Take your time.

Antony   Thou canst not fear[12] us, Pompey, with thy sails;
25   We'll speak[13] with thee at sea. At land, thou know'st
How much we do o'er-count thee.

Pompey   At land, indeed,
Thou dost o'er-count[14] me of my father's house.
But since the cuckoo builds not[15] for himself,
Remain in't as thou mayst.

Lepidus   Be pleased to tell us
30   (For this is from[16] the present) how you take
The offers we have sent you.

Caesar   There's the point.

Antony   Which do not be entreated[17] to, but weigh
What it is worth, embraced.[18]

---

7 armed rest = warlike remainder/remnant
8 wooers, those who court
9 (1) overwhelm, (2) drown in blood
10 be nothing more than
11 make ready★
12 frighten
13 deal
14 (1) outnumber, (2) cheat (Antony bought a house from Pompey's father but did not pay for it)
15 builds not: cuckoos do not build nests, only steal them
16 irrelevant to
17 begged
18 if accepted

Caesar   And what may follow,
  To try a larger fortune.[19]

Pompey   You have made me offer
  Of Sicily, Sardinia. And I must   35
  Rid all the sea of pirates. Then, to send
  Measures[20] of wheat to Rome. This 'greed upon,
  To part with unhacked edges,[21] and bear back
  Our targes undinted.[22]

Caesar, Antony, Lepidus   That's our offer.

Pompey   Know, then,
  I came before you here a man prepared   40
  To take this offer. But Mark Antony
  Put me to some impatience. (*to Anthony*) Though I lose
  The praise of it by telling, you must know
  When Caesar and your brother were at blows,
  Your mother came to Sicily and did find   45
  Her welcome friendly.

Antony   I have heard it, Pompey,
  And am well studied for a liberal[23] thanks
  Which I do owe you.

Pompey   Let me have your hand.
  I did not think, sir, to have met you here.

Antony The beds i' the east are soft, and thanks[24] to you,   50
  That call'd me timelier[25] than my purpose hither,

---

19 try a larger fortune = *either* (1) if you try for more, on your own, *or* (2) what
  may enable you, if you accept, to gain more
20 quantities
21 unhacked edges = unmangled blades/swords
22 targes undinted = shields unbeaten/undinted
23 open-hearted, abundant
24 my thanks
25 earlier

For I have gained by't.

Caesar   (to Pompey) Since I saw you last,
    There is a change upon you.

Pompey   Well, I know not
    What counts[26] harsh Fortune casts upon my face,
55   But in my bosom shall she never come,
    To make my heart her vassal.

Lepidus   Well met here.

Pompey   I hope so, Lepidus. Thus we are agreed.
    I crave our composition may be written,
    And sealed between us.

Caesar   That's the next to do.

60 Pompey   We'll feast each other ere we part, and let's
    Draw lots who shall begin.

Antony   That will I, Pompey.

Pompey   No Antony, take the lot.[27] But first or last,
    Your fine Egyptian cookery shall have
    The fame. I have heard that Julius Caesar
    Grew fat with feasting there.

65 Antony   You have heard much.

Pompey   I have fair[28] meanings, sir.

Antony   And fair words to them.

Pompey   Then so much have I heard,
    And I have heard, Apollodorus[29] carried –

Enobarbus No more of that. He did so.

Pompey   What, I pray you?

26 (1) reckonings, answering for my behavior, (2) tales, stories
27 take the lot = accept the results of drawing lots
28 attractive
29 apoloDOrus

Enobarbus A certain queen[30] to Caesar in a mattress.   70

Pompey   I know thee now. How far'st thou,[31] soldier?

Enobarbus   Well,

    And well am like to do, for I perceive

    Four feasts are toward.[32]

Pompey   Let me shake thy hand,

    I never hated thee. I have seen thee fight,

    When I have envied[33] thy behavior.

Enobarbus   Sir,   75

    I never loved you much, but I ha' praised ye,

    When you have well deserved ten times as much

    As I have said you did.

Pompey   Enjoy thy plainness,[34]

    It nothing ill becomes thee.

    Aboard my galley I invite you all.   80

    Will you lead, lords?

Caesar, Antony, Lepidus   Show us the way, sir.

Pompey   Come.

EXEUNT ALL BUT MENAS AND ENOBARBUS

Menas   (*aside*) Thy father, Pompey, would ne'er have made
    this treaty. (*to Enobarbus*) You and I have known,[35] sir.

Enobarbus At sea, I think.

Menas   We have, sir.   85

---

30 Cleopatra had gotten into Caesar's quarters by hiding herself inside a roll of
   bedding
31 how far'st thou = how are you, how are you doing ("fare")
32 coming (TAWwood)
33 regretted/regarded with disfavor
34 frankness, bluntness
35 have known = are known to each other

Enobarbus You have done well by water.

Menas And you by land.

Enobarbus I will praise any man that will praise me, though it cannot be denied what I have done by land.

90 *Menas* Nor what I have done by water.

Enobarbus Yes, something you can deny for your own safety. You have been a great thief by sea.

Menas And you by land.

Enobarbus There I deny my land service. But give me your
95 hand, Menas. If our eyes had authority,[36] here they might take[37] two thieves kissing.[38]

Menas All men's faces are true, whatsome'er their hands are.

Enobarbus But there is never a fair woman has a true face.

Menas No[39] slander, they steal hearts.

100 *Enobarbus* We came hither to fight with you.

Menas For my part, I am sorry it is turned to a drinking. Pompey doth this day laugh away his fortune.

Enobarbus If he do, sure he cannot weep't back again.

Menas You've said, sir. We looked not for Mark Antony here.
105 Pray you, is he married to Cleopatra?

Enobarbus Caesar's sister is called Octavia.

Menas True sir, she was the wife of Caius[40] Marcellus.

Enobarbus But she is now the wife of Marcus Antonius.

Menas Pray ye, sir?

110 *Enobarbus* 'Tis true.

36 power (here, as policemen)
37 seize, capture
38 associating, fraternizing
39 that is no
40 CEYoos

Menas   Then is Caesar and he for ever knit together.

Enobarbus If I were bound to divine[41] of this unity, I would not prophesy so.

Menas   I think the policy of that purpose made[42] more in the marriage than the love of the parties.   115

Enobarbus I think so too. But you shall find, the band that seems to tie their friendship together will be the very strangler of their amity: Octavia is of a holy, cold, and still conversation.[43]

Menas   Who would not have his wife so?

Enobarbus Not he that himself is not so! Which is Mark Antony. 120 He will to his Egyptian dish again. Then shall the sighs of Octavia blow the fire up in Caesar and (as I said before) that which is the strength of their amity shall prove the immediate author of their variance. Antony will use his affection where it is. He married but his occasion[44] here.   125

Menas   And thus it may be. Come, sir, will you aboard? I have a health[45] for you.

Enobarbus I shall take it, sir. We have used our throats in Egypt.

Menas   Come, let's away.

EXEUNT

41 guess, conjecture
42 weighed, counted
43 (1) intimacy, in general, (2) intimacy, specifically sexual
44 but his occasion = only his circumstances
45 toast, drink

73

SCENE 7

On board Pompey's galley, off Misenum

MUSIC

ENTER SERVANTS WITH A BANQUET[1]

Servant 1 Here they'll be, man. Some o' their plants[2] are ill
    rooted already. The least wind i' the world will blow them
    down.

Servant 2 Lepidus is high-colored.

5 *Servant 1* They have made him drink alms-drink.[3]

Servant 2 As they pinch[4] one another by the disposition,[5] he
    cries out, "No more,"[6] reconciles them to his entreaty, and
    himself to the drink.

Servant 1 But it raises the greater war between him and his
10   discretion.

Servant 2 Why, this is to have a name in great men's fellowship.[7]
    I had as lief have a reed that will do me no service as a
    partisan[8] I could not heave.[9]

Servant 1 To be called into a huge sphere, and not to be seen to
15   move in't, are[10] the holes where eyes should be, which
    pitifully disaster[11] the cheeks.

---

1 sweets, fruit, and wine
2 pun on "feet" (i.e., the banqueters are already getting drunk)
3 toasts drunk to soothe over quarrels
4 squeeze, nip, snap, harass
5 by the disposition = because of their differing/antagonistic natures
6 no more = no more quarreling
7 comradeship*
8 spear with a long handle
9 (1) lift, (2) throw
10 are like
11 spoil, ruin

A SENNET[12]

ENTER CAESAR, ANTONY, LEPIDUS, POMPEY, AGRIPPA,
MAECENAS, ENOBARBUS, MENAS, WITH OTHER COMMANDERS

Antony   (*to Caesar*) Thus do they sir. They take[13] the flow o'
the Nile
By certain scales i' th' pyramid.[14] They know,
By th' height, the lowness, or the mean, if dearth
Or foison[15] follow. The higher Nilus swells,   20
The more it promises. As it ebbs, the seedsman
Upon the slime and ooze scatters his grain,
And shortly[16] comes to harvest.

Lepidus   Y' have strange serpents there?

Antony   Ay Lepidus.   25

Lepidus   Your serpent of Egypt is bred now of your mud by
the operation of your sun. So is your crocodile.

Antony   They are so.

Pompey   Sit – and some wine! A health to Lepidus!

Lepidus   I am not so well as I should be, but I'll ne'er out.[17]   30

Enobarbus Not till you have slept. I fear me you'll be in[18] till then.

Lepidus   Nay certainly, I have heard the Ptolemies' pyramises[19]
are very goodly things. Without contradiction, I have heard
that.

12 trumpet fanfare
13 measure
14 scales i' th' pyramid = graded measurements on a stone object of pyramid
shape set in the Nile
15 dearth or foison = scarcity or plenty (FOYzen)
16 in a short time, quickly
17 stand out, refuse
18 in liquor (?)
19 pyramids: Lepidus is drunk

35 *Menas* (*aside to Pompey*) Pompey, a word.

Pompey (*aside to Menas*) Say in mine ear. What is't?

Menas (*aside to Pompey*) Forsake thy seat, I do beseech thee, captain,

And hear me speak a word.

40 *Pompey* (*aside to Menas*) Forbear me till anon.[20]

(*aloud*) This wine for Lepidus!

Lepidus What manner o' thing is your crocodile?

Antony It is shaped sir, like itself, and it is as broad as it hath breadth. It is just so high as it is, and moves with its own

45 organs. It lives by that which nourisheth it, and the elements[21] once out of it, it transmigrates.[22]

Lepidus What color is it of?

Antony Of it own color too.

Lepidus 'Tis a strange serpent.

50 *Antony* 'Tis so. And the tears of it are wet.

Caesar Will this description satisfy him?

Antony With the health[23] that Pompey gives him, else he is a very epicure.[24]

Pompey (*aside to Menas*) Go hang,[25] sir, hang! Tell me of that?

55 Away!

Do as I bid you. (*aloud*) Where's this cup I called for?

Menas (*aside to Pompey*) If for the sake of merit thou wilt hear me,

Rise from thy stool.

20 a little while
21 component parts
22 passes on
23 toast
24 a glutton (for information)
25 hang yourself

Pompey (*aside to Menas*) I think thou'rt mad. (*rises, walks aside*)   60
    The matter?

Menas   I have ever held my cap off [26] to thy fortunes.

Pompey   Thou hast served me with much faith. What's else to
    say?

    (*to the others*) Be jolly, lords.

Antony   These quick-sands, Lepidus,   65
    Keep off them, for you sink.

Menas   Wilt thou be lord of all the world?

Pompey   What say'st thou?

Menas   Wilt thou be lord of the whole world? That's twice.

Pompey   How should that be?

Menas   But entertain [27] it,
    And though thou think me poor, [28] I am the man   70
    Will give thee all the world.

Pompey   Hast thou drunk well?

Menas   No Pompey, I have kept me from the cup.
    Thou art, if thou dar'st be, the earthly Jove.
    Whate'er the ocean pales, [29] or sky inclips, [30]
    Is thine, if thou wilt ha't.

Pompey   Show me which way.   75

Menas   These three world-sharers, these competitors,
    Are in thy vessel. Let me cut the cable,
    And when we are put off, fall [31] to their throats.
    All there is thine.

26 held my cap off = been deferential/respectful
27 consider
28 deficient
29 encircles, fences in
30 encloses
31 take ("cut")

Pompey	Ah, this thou shouldst have done,

80   And not have spoke on't! In me 'tis villainy,

In thee't had been good service. Thou must know,

'Tis not my profit that does lead mine honor.

Mine honor, it. Repent that e'er thy tongue

Hath so betrayed thine act. Being done unknown,

85   I should have found it afterwards well done,

But must condemn it now. Desist, and drink.

Menas   (*aside*) For this,

I'll never follow thy palled[32] fortunes more.

Who seeks, and will not take when once 'tis offered,

Shall never find it more.

90 *Pompey*   This health to Lepidus!

Antony   Bear him ashore. I'll pledge it for him, Pompey.

Enobarbus   Here's to thee, Menas!

Menas   Enobarbus, welcome!

Pompey   Fill till the cup be hid.

Enobarbus   (*pointing to Attendant carrying off Lepidus*) There's a

strong fellow, Menas.

95 *Menas*   Why?

Enobarbus   A'[33] bears the third part of the world, man. See'st

not?

Menas   The third part, then, is drunk. Would it were all,

That it might go on wheels![34]

Enobarbus   Drink thou. Increase the reels.[35]

100 *Menas*   Come.[36]

32 enfeebled, weakened
33 he
34 go on wheels = spin wildly (?) go fast (?)
35 staggering
36 (?) disagreement? agreement? invitation?

Pompey   This is not yet an Alexandrian[37] feast.

Antony   It ripens towards it. Strike the vessels,[38] ho!

    Here is to Caesar!

Caesar   I could well forbear't.

    It's monstrous labor when I wash my brain

    And it grows fouler.

Antony   Be a child o' the time.   105

Caesar   Possess it, I'll make answer.[39]

    But I had rather fast from all,[40] four days,

    Than drink so much in one.

Enobarbus   Ha, my brave emperor!

    (*to Antony*) Shall we dance now the Egyptian bacchanals,[41]

    And celebrate our drink?

Pompey   Let's ha't, good soldier.   110

Antony   Come, let's all take hands,

    Till that the conquering wine hath steeped our sense

    In soft and delicate Lethe.

Enobarbus   All take hands.

    Make battery to our ears with the loud music,

    The while I'll place[42] you. Then the boy shall sing.   115

    The holding[43] every man shall bear[44] as loud

    As his strong sides can volley.[45]

---

37 Alexandria was the second city in the Roman Empire, second only to Rome itself

38 strike the vessels = open more wine casks

39 (?) possess it, I'll make answer = when you possess the time, then I'll answer you

40 everything

41 drunken celebration of Bacchus, the god of wine

42 position

43 refrain, burden

44 carry, sing

45 utter, discharge

MUSIC

ENOBARBUS PLACES THEM HAND IN HAND, AND THEY SING

> Come, thou monarch of the vine,
> Plumpy Bacchus with pink eyne!
120   In thy fats[46] our cares be drowned,
> With thy grapes our hairs be crowned.
>> Cup us, till the world go round,
>> Cup us, till the world go round!

Caesar   What would you more? Pompey, good night. Good brother,
125   Let me request you off.[47] Our graver business
Frowns at this levity. Gentle lords, let's part.
You see we have burnt our cheeks. Strong Enobarb
Is weaker than the wine, and mine own tongue
Splits what it speaks. The wild disguise[48] hath almost
130   Anticked[49] us all. What needs more words? Good night.
Good Antony, your hand.

Pompey   I'll try you[50] on the shore.

Antony   And shall sir, give's your hand.

Pompey   O Antony,
You have my father's house. But what,[51] we are friends!
Come, down into the boat.

Enobarbus   Take heed you fall not.

46 vessels, casks ("vats")
47 you off = you leave the galley with me
48 disorder because of drinking
49 made grotesques of us
50 try you = test★ your drinking capabilities
51 so what

EXEUNT ALL BUT ENOBARBUS AND MENAS

    Menas, I'll not[52] on shore.

Menas   No, to my cabin.   135

    These drums, these trumpets, flutes! What,

    Let Neptune[53] hear we bid a loud farewell

    To these great fellows. Sound and be hanged, sound out!

FLOURISH, WITH DRUMS

Enobarbus Ho, says a'. (*throwing his cap*) There's my cap.

Menas   Ho! Noble captain, come.   140

EXEUNT

---

52 I'll not = don't want/will not go
53 god of the sea★

Act 3

SCENE I

A plain in Syria

ENTER VENTIDIUS, TRIUMPHANTLY, WITH SILIUS,
AND OTHER ROMANS, OFFICERS, AND SOLDIERS;
THE DEAD BODY OF PACORUS[1] BORNE BEFORE HIM

Ventidius Now darting[2] Parthia art thou stroke,[3] and now
　　　Pleased fortune does of Marcus Crassus' death[4]
　　　Make me revenger. Bear the king's son's body
　　　Before our army. Thy Pacorus, Orodes,[5]
　　　Pays this for Marcus Crassus.

5　*Silius*　　　　　　　　　　Noble Ventidius,
　　　Whilst yet with Parthian blood thy sword is warm,
　　　The fugitive Parthians follow.[6] Spur[7] through Media,[8]

1 son of Orodes, king of Parthia
2 dart-shooting (then quickly running away)
3 struck, stricken
4 in Parthia, Marcus Crassus having been (with Julius Caesar and Pompey) one
　of the first three triumvirs
5 oROWdeez
6 the fugitive Parthians follow = follow the fugitive Parthians
7 hasten, hurry, proceed urgently
8 country SW of Caspian Sea

Mesopotamia, and the shelters whither
The routed[9] fly. So thy grand captain Antony
Shall set thee on triumphant chariots and   10
Put garlands on thy head.
Ventidius   O Silius, Silius,
I have done enough. A lower place (note well)
May make too great an act. For learn this, Silius,
Better to leave undone, than by our deed
Acquire too high a fame when him we serve's away.   15
Caesar and Antony have ever won
More in their officer than person. Sossius,
One of my place in Syria, his[10] lieutenant,
For quick accumulation of renown
(Which he achieved by the minute) lost his favor.   20
Who does i' the wars more than his captain can
Becomes his captain's captain. And ambition,
The soldier's virtue, rather makes choice of loss
Than gain which darkens him.[11]
I could do more to do Antonius good,   25
But 'twould offend him. And in his offense
Should my performance perish.
Silius   Thou hast, Ventidius, that[12]
Without the which a soldier, and his sword,
Grants scarce distinction.[13] Thou wilt write to Antony.
Ventidius I'll humbly signify what in his name,   30
That magical word of war, we have effected,

9 those who have been routed/defeated
10 Antony's
11 darkens him = obscures his captain
12 i.e., discretion
13 grants scarce distinction = permits hardly any difference to be seen, as
between soldier and sword

How with his banners and his well-paid ranks
The ne'er-yet-beaten horse[14] of Parthia
We have jaded[15] out o' the field.

Silius   Where is he now?

35 *Ventidius* He purposeth to Athens, whither (with what haste
The weight we must convey with's[16] will permit)
We shall appear before him. (*to Soldiers*) On there, pass along!

EXEUNT

14 cavalry
15 exhausted, worn down
16 convey with's = take/lead/carry with us

SCENE 2

Rome, an antechamber in Caesar's house

ENTER AGRIPPA AT ONE DOOR, ENOBARBUS AT ANOTHER

Agrippa   What, are the brothers parted?[1]

Enobarbus They have dispatched with[2] Pompey, he is gone,
    The other three are sealing. Octavia weeps
    To part from Rome. Caesar is sad, and Lepidus,
    Since Pompey's feast, as Menas says, is troubled   5
    With the green sickness.[3]

Agrippa   'Tis a noble Lepidus.

Enobarbus A very fine one. O, how he loves Caesar!

Agrippa   Nay, but how dearly he adores Mark Antony!

Enobarbus Caesar? Why, he's the Jupiter of men.

Agrippa   What's Antony? The god of Jupiter?   10

Enobarbus Spake you of Caesar? How, the non-pareil?[4]

Agrippa   O Antony, O thou Arabian bird![5]

Enobarbus Would you praise Caesar, say "Caesar." Go no further.

Agrippa   Indeed, he plied[6] them both with excellent praises.

Enobarbus But he loves Caesar best, yet he loves Antony.   15
    Ho, hearts, tongues, figures, scribes, bards, poets, cannot
    Think, speak, cast,[7] write, sing, number, ho!
    His love to Antony. But as for Caesar,

1 (1) separated, (2) departed
2 dispatched with = sent away, disposed of
3 green sickness = anemia thought to be caused in young girls by love
4 peerless (nonpaREL)
5 Arabian bird = the phoenix, mythological self-recreating creature (i.e.,
    utterly unique)
6 covered
7 calculate, reckon up

Kneel down, kneel down, and wonder.

Agrippa   Both he loves.

20 *Enobarbus* They are his shards,[8] and he their beetle, so.

TRUMPETS WITHIN

This is to horse. Adieu, noble Agrippa.

Agrippa   Good fortune, worthy soldier, and farewell.

ENTER CAESAR, ANTONY, LEPIDUS, AND OCTAVIA

Antony   No further, sir.

Caesar   You take from me a great part of myself.

25   Use[9] me well in 't. Sister, prove such a wife
As my thoughts make thee, and as my farthest band[10]
Shall pass on thy approof.[11] Most noble Antony,
Let not the piece of virtue which is set
Betwixt us as the cement[12] of our love,
30   To keep it builded, be the ram to batter
The fortress of it. For better might we
Have loved without this mean,[13] if on both parts
This be not cherished.

Antony   Make me not offended
In[14] your distrust.

Caesar   I have said.

Antony   You shall not find,

---

  8 wings
  9 treat
 10 farthest band = greatest pledge ("bond")
 11 pass on thy approof = you will prove to surpass
 12 SEEment
 13 intermediary
 14 by

Though you be therein curious,[15] the least cause   35
For what you seem to fear. So the gods keep you,
And make the hearts of Romans serve your ends!
We will here part.

Caesar   Farewell, my dearest sister, fare thee well.
The elements be kind to thee, and make   40
Thy spirits all of comfort. Fare thee well.

Octavia   My noble brother!

Antony   The April's in her eyes. It is love's spring,
And these the showers to bring it on. Be cheerful.

Octavia   Sir, look well to my husband's house, and –   45

Caesar   What, Octavia?

Octavia   I'll tell you in your ear.

Antony   Her tongue will not obey her heart, nor can
Her heart inform[16] her tongue – the swan's-down feather,[17]
That stands[18] upon the swell at full of tide,
And neither way[19] inclines.   50

Enobarbus (*aside*) Will Caesar weep?

Agrippa   (*aside*) He has a cloud[20] in 's
face.

Enobarbus (*aside*) He were the worse for that, were he a horse.
So is he, being a man.

Agrippa   (*aside*) Why, Enobarbus,
When Antony found Julius Caesar dead,[21]   55

15 anxious
16 animate, shape
17 i.e., her tongue is like the soft feather
18 floats
19 i.e., toward neither her brother nor her husband
20 (1) troubling mark, (2) on a horse, a dark and undesirable spot
21 when ANtoNY found JULyus CAEsar DEAD

He cried almost to roaring. And he wept
When at Philippi he found Brutus slain.

Enobarbus (*aside*) That year, indeed, he was troubled with a
rheum.[22]

What willingly he did confound he wailed,
Believe't, till I weep too.

60 *Caesar*   No, sweet Octavia,
You shall hear from me still.[23] The time shall not
Outgo[24] my thinking on you.

Antony   Come sir, come,
I'll wrestle with you in my strength of love.
(*embraces Caesar*) Look, here I have you. Thus I let you go,
And give you to the gods.

65 *Caesar*   Adieu, be happy.

Lepidus   Let all the number of the stars give light
To thy fair way!

Caesar   (*kissing Octavia*) Farewell, farewell!

Antony   Farewell!

TRUMPETS

EXEUNT

22 affliction causing watery matter in the eyes
23 always
24 outdistance, run away from

SCENE 3
Alexandria, Cleopatra's palace

ENTER CLEOPATRA, CHARMIAN, IRAS, AND ALEXAS

Cleopatra Where is the fellow?
Alexas   Half afeard to come.
Cleopatra Go to, go to.

ENTER THE MESSENGER, NERVOUS AS BEFORE

                         Come hither, sir.
Alexas   Good majesty,
   Herod of Jewry dare not[1] look upon you
   But when you are well pleased.
Cleopatra   That Herod's head
   I'll have. But how? When Antony is gone   5
   Through whom I might command it. (*to Messenger*) Come
   thou near.
Messenger Most gracious majesty –
Cleopatra Didst thou behold Octavia?
Messenger   Ay, dread queen.
Cleopatra Where?
Messenger   Madam, in Rome.
   I looked her in the face, and saw her led   10
   Between her brother and Mark Antony.
Cleopatra Is she as tall as me?
Messenger   She is not, madam.
Cleopatra Didst hear her speak? Is she shrill-tongued or low?
Messenger Madam, I heard her speak, she is low-voiced.

---

1 dare not = would not dare

15 *Cleopatra*   That's not so good. He cannot like her long.

   Charmian   Like her? O Isis, 'tis impossible.

   Cleopatra   I think so, Charmian. Dull of tongue, and dwarfish!

   What majesty is in her gait? Remember,

   If e'er thou look'dst on majesty.

   Messenger   She creeps.[2]

20 Her motion and her station[3] are as one.

   She shows a body rather than a life,

   A statue than a breather.

   Cleopatra   Is this certain?

   Messenger   Or I have no observance.[4]

   Charmian   Three in Egypt

   Cannot make better note.[5]

   Cleopatra   He's very knowing,

25 I do perceive't. There's nothing in her yet.

   The fellow has good judgment.

   Charmian   Excellent.

   Cleopatra   Guess at her years, I prithee.

   Messenger   Madam,

   She was a widow –

   Cleopatra   Widow! Charmian, hark.

   Messenger   And I do think she's thirty.

30 *Cleopatra*   Bear'st thou her face in mind?[6] Is't long or round?

   Messenger   Round even to faultiness.

   Cleopatra   For the most part, too, they are foolish that are so.

---

2 moves softly / timorously / slowly
3 standing posture
4 capacity of observation
5 i.e., there are not three people in Egypt who can observe better than this
   messenger
6 your memory

Her hair, what color?

Messenger   Brown, madam, and her forehead
    As low as she would wish it.

Cleopatra   (*gives him money*) There's gold
    for thee.
    Thou must not take my former sharpness ill,   35
    I will employ thee back again, I find thee
    Most fit⁷ for business. Go, make thee ready,
    Our letters are prepared.

EXIT MESSENGER

Charmian   A proper⁸ man.

Cleopatra Indeed he is so. I repent me much
    That so I harried⁹ him. Why methinks by him,   40
    This creature's no such thing.¹⁰

Charmian   Nothing, madam.

Cleopatra The man hath seen some majesty, and should know.

Charmian Hath he seen majesty? Isis else defend,¹¹
    And serving you so long!

Cleopatra I have one thing more to ask him yet, good
    Charmian.   45
    But 'tis no matter, thou shalt bring him to me
    Where I will write. All may be well enough.

Charmian I warrant you, madam.

EXEUNT

7 suited★
8 accurate, correct
9 harassed, maltreated
10 no such thing = nothing much
11 forbid

SCENE 4

Athens, a room in Antony's house

ENTER ANTONY AND OCTAVIA

Antony Nay, nay, Octavia, not only that –
That were excusable, that and thousands more
Of semblable import[1] – but he hath waged
New wars 'gainst Pompey. Made his will, and read it
5 To public ear.
Spoke scantly[2] of me, when perforce[3] he could not
But pay me terms of honor. Cold and sickly
He vented them.[4] Most narrow measure[5] lent me.
When the best hint was given him, he not took't,
Or did it from[6] his teeth.
10 *Octavia*   O my good lord,
Believe not all, or if you must believe,
Stomach[7] not all. A more unhappy lady,
If this division chance,[8] ne'er stood between,
Praying for both parts.
15 The good gods will mock me presently,
When I shall pray, "O bless my lord and husband,"
Undo that prayer, by crying out as loud,
"O bless my brother!" Husband win, win brother,

---

1 semblable import = much the same significance
2 barely, scarcely
3 of necessity
4 vented them = came out with those terms of honor
5 quantity, value
6 through
7 resent, be offended at
8 (verb) happen, come about

Prays, and destroys the prayer. No midway
'Twixt these extremes at all.

Antony   Gentle Octavia,   20
    Let your best love draw to that point which seeks
    Best to preserve it. If I lose mine honor,
    I lose myself. Better I were not yours
    Than yours so branchless.[9] But as you requested,
    Yourself shall go between 's. The meantime, lady,   25
    I'll raise the preparation of a war
    Shall stain[10] your brother. Make your soonest haste,
    So[11] your desires are yours.

Octavia   Thanks to my lord.
    The Jove of power make me (most weak, most weak)
    Your reconciler! Wars 'twixt you twain would be   30
    As if the world should cleave, and that slain men
    Should solder up the rift.

Antony   When it appears to you where this begins,
    Turn your displeasure that way, for our faults
    Can never be so equal that your love   35
    Can equally move with them. Provide your going,[12]
    Choose your own company, and command what cost
    Your heart has mind to.

EXEUNT

9 destitute
10 throw into the shade
11 as long as
12 to Rome, to confer with her brother

SCENE 5

Athens, a room in Antony's house

ENTER ENOBARBUS AND EROS

Enobarbus	How now, friend Eros!
Eros	There's strange news come, sir.
Enobarbus	What, man?
Eros	Caesar and Lepidus have made wars upon Pompey.

5 *Enobarbus* This is old, what is the success?[1]

Eros Caesar, having made use of him[2] in the wars 'gainst
Pompey, presently denied him rivality,[3] would not let him
partake in the glory of the action, and not resting here,
accuses him of letters he had formerly wrote to Pompey.

10 Upon his[4] own appeal,[5] seizes him, so the poor third is up,[6]
till death enlarge his confine.[7]

Enobarbus Then would thou hast a pair of chaps,[8] no more,
And throw between them all the food thou hast,
They'll grind the one the other. Where's Antony?

15 *Eros* He's walking in the garden – thus, and spurns
The rush[9] that lies before him, cries, "Fool Lepidus!"
And threats the throat of that his[10] officer
That murdered Pompey.

---

1 upshot/sequel/result
2 Lepidus
3 equality
4 Caesar's
5 charge
6 (1) finished, played out, (2) in custody
7 boundaries, enclosure
8 jaws
9 spurns the rush = kicks the reeds/plants
10 Antony's

Enobarbus	Our great navy's rigged.
Eros	For Italy and Caesar. More, Domitius.

My lord desires you presently. My news   20
I might have told hereafter.

Enobarbus	'Twill be naught,[11]

But let it be. Bring me to Antony.

Eros	Come sir.

EXEUNT

11 nothing, a matter of no importance

SCENE 6
Rome, Caesar's house

ENTER CAESAR, AGRIPPA, AND MAECENAS

Caesar Contemning[1] Rome, he has done all this, and more,
   In Alexandria. Here's the manner of 't.
   I' the market-place, on a tribunal[2] silvered,
   Cleopatra and himself in chairs of gold
5   Were publicly enthroned. At the feet sat
   Caesarion, whom they call my father's[3] son,
   And all the unlawful issue that their lust
   Since then hath made between them. Unto her
   He gave the stablishment[4] of Egypt, made her
10   Of lower Syria, Cyprus, Lydia,
   Absolute queen.

Maecenas   This in the public eye?

Caesar I' the common show-place, where they exercise,[5]
   His sons hither[6] proclaimed the kings of kings.
   Great Media, Parthia, and Armenia
15   He gave to Alexander. To Ptolemy he assigned
   Syria, Cilicia, and Phoenicia. She[7]
   In the habiliments of the goddess Isis
   That day appeared, and oft before gave audience,

---

1 disdaining, scorning
2 platform, dais
3 Julius Caesar, his father by adoption (Octavius was in fact Julius Caesar's grandnephew); Caesarion was Julius Caesar's child
4 confirmed possession
5 perform military drills
6 recently
7 Cleopatra

As 'tis reported, so.

Maecenas   Let Rome be thus informed.

Agrippa   Who queasy with his insolence   20
  Already, will their good thoughts call from him.

Caesar   The people knows it, and have now received
  His accusations.

Agrippa   Who does he accuse?

Caesar   Caesar, and that, having in Sicily
  Sextus Pompeius spoiled,[8] we had not rated[9] him   25
  His part o' the isle. Then does he say, he lent me
  Some shipping unrestored. Lastly, he frets[10]
  That Lepidus of the triumvirate
  Should be deposed, and being that, we detain[11]
  All his revenue.[12]

Agrippa   Sir, this should be answered.   30

Caesar   'Tis done already, and the messenger gone.
  I have told him Lepidus was grown too cruel,
  That he his high authority abused,
  And did deserve his change.[13] For what I have conquered,
  I grant him part, but then, in his Armenia,   35
  And other of his conquered kingdoms, I
  Demand the like.

Maecenas   He'll never yield to that.

Caesar   Nor must not then be yielded to in this.

---

  8 despoiled, stripped
  9 assigned
  10 is distressed
  11 have held back★
  12 his revenue = Antony's moneys (reVENyou)
  13 (1) alteration, (2) death

ENTER OCTAVIA WITH HER ATTENDANTS

	Octavia	Hail, Caesar, and my lord, hail, most dear Caesar!
40	Caesar	That ever I should call thee cast away!
	Octavia	You have not called me so, nor have you cause.
	Caesar	Why have you stol'n upon us thus? You come not

Like Caesar's sister. The wife of Antony
Should have an army for an usher,[14] and
45 The neighs of horse to tell of her approach
Long ere she did appear. The trees by the way
Should have borne men, and expectation fainted,
Longing for what it had not. Nay, the dust
Should have ascended to the roof of heaven,
50 Raised by your populous troops. But you are come
A market-maid to Rome, and have prevented[15]
The ostentation[16] of our[17] love, which left unshown,
Is often left unloved. We should have met you
By sea and land, supplying every stage[18]
With an augmented greeting.

55 Octavia   Good my lord,
To come thus was I not constrained,[19] but did
On my free will. My lord, Mark Antony,
Hearing that you prepared for war, acquainted
My grieved ear withal. Whereon I begged
His pardon[20] for return.

14 someone who goes in advance and announces the honored person's coming
15 outrun, made useless
16 display, exhibition, show
17 Caesar's
18 step along the way
19 compelled, forced★
20 permission

Caesar   Which soon he granted,   60
  Being an obstruct[21] 'tween his lust and him.
Octavia Do not say so, my lord.
Caesar   I have eyes upon him,
  And his affairs come to me on the wind.
  Where is he now?
Octavia   My lord, in Athens.
Caesar   No, my most wronged sister, Cleopatra   65
  Hath nodded[22] him to her. He hath given his empire
  Up to a whore, who now are levying
  The kings o' the earth for war. He hath assembled
  Bocchus the King of Libya, Archelaus
  Of Cappadocia, Philadelphos King   70
  Of Paphlagonia, the Thracian king Adallas,
  King Manchus of Arabia, King of Pont,
  Herod of Jewry, Mithridates King
  Of Comagene, Polemon and Amyntas,
  The Kings of Mede and Lycaonia,   75
  With a more larger list of scepters.
Octavia   Ay me, most wretched,
  That have my heart parted betwixt two friends
  That do afflict each other!
Caesar   Welcome hither.
  Your letters did withhold[23] our breaking forth
  Till we perceived both how you were wrong led,   80
  And we in negligent danger. Cheer your heart,
  Be you not troubled with the time, which drives

21 obstruction
22 commanded, invited (with a nod)
23 restrain, check★

99

O'er your content[24] these strong necessities,
But let determined things to destiny
85   Hold unbewailed their way. Welcome to Rome,
Nothing more dear to me. You are abused
Beyond the mark[25] of thought. And the high gods
To do you justice makes his ministers
Of us[26] and those that love you. Best of comfort
And ever welcome to us.

90 *Agrippa*   Welcome lady.

Maecenas Welcome, dear madam.
Each heart in Rome does love and pity you.
Only the adulterous Antony, most large
In his abominations, turns you off,[27]
95   And gives his potent regiment[28] to a trull[29]
That noises it[30] against us.

Octavia   Is it so sir?

Caesar   Most certain. Sister, welcome. Pray you,
Be ever known to[31] patience. My dear'st sister.

EXEUNT

24 conTENT
25 boundary
26 his ministers of us = us/me his ministers (Elizabethan usage differs from
    contemporary usage, in singular and plural forms)
27 away
28 authority
29 whore
30 noises it = cries it out
31 known to = familiar with

SCENE 7

Near Actium,[1] *Antony's camp*

ENTER CLEOPATRA AND ENOBARBUS

Cleopatra I will be even with thee, doubt it not.

Enobarbus But why, why, why?

Cleopatra Thou hast forspoke[2] my being in these wars,
And say'st it is not fit.

Enobarbus   Well, is it, is it?

Cleopatra If not denounced[3] against us,[4] why should not we   5
Be there in person?

Enobarbus   (*aside*) Well, I could reply.
If we should serve with horse and mares together,
The horse were merely[5] lost. The mares would bear
A soldier and his horse.

Cleopatra   What is't you say?

Enobarbus Your presence needs must puzzle[6] Antony,   10
Take from his heart, take from his brain, from's time,
What should not then be spared. He is already
Traduced[7] for levity, and 'tis said in Rome
That Photinus[8] an eunuch and your maids
Manage this war.

Cleopatra   Sink Rome, and their tongues rot   15

1 promontory in W Greece (ACKteeum)
2 forbidden, spoken against
3 officially proclaimed/announced
4 the royal "we," meaning "me"
5 absolutely
6 confound, embarrass, bewilder
7 censured, defamed, maligned
8 (?) this should perhaps be Mardian: this eunuch has no other mention in the
  play

That speak against us! A charge[9] we bear i' the war,
And as the president[10] of my kingdom, will
Appear there for[11] a man. Speak not against it:
I will not stay behind.

Enobarbus   Nay I have done.
Here comes the Emperor.

ENTER ANTONY AND CANIDIUS[12]

20 *Antony*   Is it not strange, Canidius,
That from Tarentum and Brundusium
He could so quickly cut[13] the Ionian sea,
And take in[14] Toryne? You have heard on't, sweet?

Cleopatra Celerity is never more admired
Than by the negligent.

25 *Antony*   A good rebuke,
Which might have well becomed the best of men,
To taunt at slackness. Canidius, we
Will fight with him by sea.

Cleopatra   By sea, what else?

Canidius Why will my lord do so?

Antony   For that he dares us to't.

30 *Enobarbus* So hath my lord dared him to single fight.

Canidius Ay, and to wage this battle at Pharsalia,
Where Caesar fought with Pompey. But these offers,
Which serve not for his vantage, he shakes off,

9 burden, responsibility, expense
10 presiding officer, head
11 in place of
12 caNIdeeus
13 pass through, cross
14 take in = capture, conquer

And so should you.

Enobarbus   Your ships are not well manned.
   Your mariners are muleters,[15] reapers, people   35
   Ingrossed[16] by swift impress.[17] In Caesar's fleet
   Are those that often have 'gainst Pompey fought.
   Their ships are yare, yours heavy. No disgrace
   Shall fall you for refusing him at sea,
   Being prepared for land.

Antony   By sea, by sea.   40

Enobarbus Most worthy sir, you therein throw away
   The absolute soldiership[18] you have by land,
   Distract[19] your army, which doth most consist
   Of war-marked footmen,[20] leave unexecuted[21]
   Your own renownèd knowledge, quite forego   45
   The way which promises assurance, and
   Give up yourself merely to chance and hazard,
   From[22] firm security.

Antony   I'll fight at sea.

Cleopatra I have sixty sails, Caesar none better.

Antony   Our overplus[23] of shipping will we burn,   50
   And with the rest full-manned, from th' head[24] of Actium
   Beat the approaching Caesar. But if we fail,

15 mule drivers
16 gathered, collected
17 enforced service
18 military experience/skill
19 confuse, divide
20 infantry
21 unused
22 instead of
23 surplus
24 foremost part

We then can do't at land.

ENTER A MESSENGER

Thy business?

Messenger   The news is true, my lord, he is descried,[25]

55   Caesar has taken Toryne.

Antony   Can he be there in person? 'Tis impossible
        Strange that his power[26] should be. Canidius,
        Our nineteen legions[27] thou shalt hold by land,
        And our twelve thousand horse. We'll to our ship.
        Away, my Thetis![28]

ENTER A SOLDIER

60   How now, worthy soldier?

Soldier   O noble emperor, do not fight by sea,
        Trust not to rotten planks. Do you misdoubt[29]
        This sword and these my wounds? Let the Egyptians
        And the Phoenicians go a-ducking.[30] We

65   Have used to conquer, standing on the earth,
        And fighting foot to foot.

Antony   Well, well, away!

EXEUNT ANTONY, CLEOPATRA, AND ENOBARBUS

Soldier   By Hercules, I think I am i' the right.

Canidius   Soldier, thou art. But his whole action grows

25 is descried = has been sighted/observed
26 army★
27 1 legion = 3,000 to 6,000 infantrymen
28 a Nereid goddess
29 mistrust
30 immersing themselves in water

Not in the power on't.[31] So our leader's led,

And we are women's men.

Soldier   You keep by land   70

The legions and the horse whole, do you not?

Canidius   Marcus Octavius, Marcus Justeius,

Publicola, and Caelius are for sea.

But we keep whole by land. This speed of Caesar's

Carries[32] beyond belief.

Soldier   While he was yet in Rome,   75

His power went out in such distractions[33] as

Beguiled[34] all spies.

Canidius   Who's his lieutenant, hear you?

Soldier   They say, one Taurus.

Canidius   Well I know the man.[35]

ENTER A MESSENGER

Messenger   The emperor calls Canidius.

Canidius   With news the time's with[36] labor, and throws forth,   80

Each minute, some.

EXEUNT

31 his whole action grows not in the power on't = everything he does is not
     based on his strength
32 is carried
33 dispersed/scattered fashion
34 deluded, deceived★
35 "I know the man well"
36 in ("labor" as in giving birth)

SCENE 8
A plain near Actium

<small>ENTER CAESAR WITH HIS ARMY, AND TAURUS</small>

Caesar Taurus.

Taurus   My lord?

Caesar Strike not by land, keep whole, provoke not battle
    Till we have done at sea. Do not exceed
    The prescript[1] of this scroll. Our fortune lies
5   Upon this jump.[2]

<small>EXEUNT</small>

---

1 command, instructions, directions
2 critical moment

SCENE 9
Another part of the plain

ENTER ANTONY AND ENOBARBUS

Antony Set we our squadrons on yond side o' the hill,
In eye[1] of Caesar's battle,[2] from which place
We may the number of the ships behold,
And so proceed accordingly.

EXEUNT

1 sight
2 formations, troops in battle array

SCENE 10

Another part of the plain

CANIDIUS MARCHES HIS ARMY ONE WAY OVER THE STAGE,
THEN TAURUS, CAESAR'S LIEUTENANT, MARCHES HIS
THE OTHER WAY. THEN WE HEAR FIRST THE NOISE
OF A SEA-FIGHT, AND THEN AN ALARUM[1]

ENTER ENOBARBUS

Enobarbus Naught, naught all, naught! I can behold[2] no longer.
Th'*Antoniad,* the Egyptian admiral,[3]
With all their sixty, fly and turn the rudder.
To see't mine eyes are blasted.[4]

ENTER SCARUS

Scarus   Gods and goddesses,
All the whole synod[5] of them!
5 *Enobarbus*   What's thy passion?
Scarus   The greater cantle[6] of the world is lost
With very ignorance, we have kissed away
Kingdoms and provinces.
Enobarbus   How appears the fight?
Scarus   On our side like the tokened[7] pestilence,
10 Where death is sure. Yon ribaudred[8] nag[9] of Egypt –

1 warning bell★
2 watch
3 flagship
4 blighted, stricken★
5 assembly
6 section, portion
7 signs/marks of
8 (?) ribald?
9 term of abuse (literally: "small pony")

Whom leprosy o'ertake! – i' the midst o' the fight,
When vantage like a pair of twins appeared
Both as the same, or rather ours the elder,[10]
The breeze[11] upon her, like a cow in June
Hoists sails and flies.

Enobarbus   That I beheld.   15
Mine eyes did sicken at the sight, and could not
Endure a further view.

Scarus   She once being loofed,[12]
The noble ruin of her magic, Antony,
Claps on his sea-wing, and (like a doting mallard)[13]
Leaving the fight in height,[14] flies after her.   20
I never saw an action of such shame.
Experience, manhood, honor, ne'er before
Did violate so itself.

Enobarbus   Alack, alack!

ENTER CANIDIUS

Canidius   Our fortune on the sea is out of breath,
And sinks most lamentably. Had our general   25
Been what he knew himself, it had gone well.
O he has given example for our flight,
Most grossly, by his own!

Enobarbus   Ay, are you thereabouts?[15]
Why then good night indeed.

10 more advanced
11 (1) gadfly, (2) wind
12 sailed with the wind ("luffed")
13 male duck
14 in height = when it was very active
15 are you thereabouts = is that what you're thinking of (i.e., flight)

30 *Canidius*   Toward Peloponnesus are they fled.

Scarus   'Tis easy to't,[16] and there I will attend[17]

What further comes.

Canidius   To Caesar will I render[18]

My legions and my horse. Six kings already

Show me the way of yielding.

Enobarbus   I'll yet follow

35 The wounded chance of Antony, though my reason

Sits in the wind against me.[19]

EXEUNT

16 (?) to get to
17 await
18 hand over
19 i.e., blows in the opposite direction

SCENE II

Alexandria, Cleopatra's palace

ENTER ANTONY, WITH ATTENDANTS

Antony Hark, the land bids me tread no more upon't,
It is ashamed to bear me. Friends, come hither,
I am so lated[1] in the world that I
Have lost my way for ever. I have a ship
Laden with gold, take that, divide it. Fly,   5
And make your peace with Caesar.

All   Fly? Not we.

Antony I have fled myself, and have instructed[2] cowards
To run and show their shoulders. Friends, be gone,
I have myself resolved upon a course   10
Which has no need of you. Be gone,
My treasure's in the harbor. Take it. O,
I followed that[3] I blush to look upon,
My very hairs do mutiny. For the white
Reprove the brown for rashness, and they them   15
For fear and doting. Friends, be gone, you shall
Have letters from me to some friends that will
Sweep[4] your way for you. Pray you look not sad,
Nor make replies of loathness,[5] take the hint
Which my despair proclaims. Let that be left   20
Which leaves itself. To the sea-side straightway.[6]

---

1 belated, out of date, overtaken by darkness
2 taught, set an example for
3 that which
4 clear
5 reluctance
6 at once*

I will possess you of that ship and treasure.

Leave me I pray, a little. Pray you now.

Nay do so, for indeed I have lost command,

25   Therefore I pray you. I'll see you by and by.[7]

ANTONY SITS DOWN

ENTER CLEOPATRA LED BY CHARMIAN
AND IRAS, EROS FOLLOWING

Eros	Nay gentle madam, to him, comfort him.
Iras	Do, most dear Queen.
Charmian	Do. Why, what else?
Cleopatra	Let me sit down. O Juno!
30 *Antony*	No, no, no, no, no.
Eros	See you here, sir?
Antony	O fie, fie, fie!
Charmian	Madam!
Iras	Madam, O good Empress!
35 *Eros*	Sir, sir –
Antony	Yes my lord, yes. He[8] at Philippi kept

His sword e'en like a dancer,[9] while I struck

The lean and wrinkled Cassius, and 'twas I

That the mad Brutus ended.[10] He alone

40   Dealt on lieutenantry,[11] and no practice had

In the brave squares[12] of war. Yet now – no matter.

7 before long, soon
8 Caesar
9 i.e., like a prop, a stage ornament
10 the mad Brutus ended = ended/finished off the mad Brutus
11 alone dealt on lieutenantry = was concerned only with strategic (as
    opposed to tactical) issues
12 (1) tools, (2) principles, (3) troop formations

Cleopatra	(*to her attendants*) Ah, stand by.[13]
Eros	The Queen, my lord, the Queen.
Iras	Go to him, madam, speak to him,

He's unqualitied[14] with very shame.   45

Cleopatra	Well then, sustain me. O!
Eros	Most noble sir arise, the Queen approaches,

Her head's declined, and death will seize[15] her, but

Your comfort makes the rescue.

Antony   I have offended[16] reputation,[17]   50

A most unnoble swerving.[18]

Eros   Sir, the Queen.

Antony   O whither hast thou led me, Egypt? See

How I convey my shame out of[19] thine eyes

By looking back[20] what I have left behind,

'Stroyed in dishonor.

Cleopatra   O my lord, my lord,   55

Forgive my fearful[21] sails! I little thought

You would have followed.

Antony   Egypt, thou knew'st too well

My heart was to thy rudder tied by the strings,

And thou shouldst tow me after. O'er my spirit

Thy full supremacy thou knew'st, and that   60

13 stand by = stay near me
14 not himself
15 Folio: cease; all editors emend
16 injured
17 i HAVE ofFENded REpyouTEYseeOWN
18 transgression
19 out of = away from
20 back at
21 timorous, frightened

Thy beck[22] might from the bidding of the gods
Command me.

Cleopatra   O my pardon!

Antony   Now I must

To the young man[23] send humble treaties, dodge
And palter[24] in the shifts[25] of lowness, who[26]
65   With half the bulk o' the world played as I pleased,
Making and marring[27] fortunes. You did know
How much you were my conqueror, and that
My sword, made weak by my affection, would
Obey it on all cause.[28]

Cleopatra   Pardon, pardon!

70   Antony   Fall not a tear I say, one of them rates[29]
All that is won and lost. Give me a kiss,
Even this repays me. We sent our schoolmaster,[30]
Is a' come back? Love, I am full of lead.
Some wine, within there, and our viands! Fortune knows
75   We scorn her most when most she offers blows.

EXEUNT

22 signal★
23 Caesar, much younger than himself
24 dodge and palter = shuffle/shift and equivocate
25 expedients
26 I who
27 ruining, spoiling★
28 on all cause = under all conditions/considerations
29 is worth
30 i.e., Euphronius, tutor to their children (youFROneeOOS), now messenger
   to Caesar

SCENE 12
Egypt, Caesar's camp

ENTER CAESAR, DOLABELLA, AND THIDIAS, WITH OTHERS

Caesar   Let him appear that's come from Antony.
  Know you him?
Dolabella   Caesar, 'tis his schoolmaster.
  An argument that he is plucked,[1] when hither
  He sends so poor a pinion[2] off his wing,
  Which had superfluous[3] kings for messengers   5
  Not many moons gone by.

ENTER EUPHRONIUS, AMBASSADOR FROM ANTONY

Caesar   Approach, and speak.
Euphronius Such as I am, I come from Antony.
  I was of late as petty to his ends
  As is the morn-dew on the myrtle-leaf
  To his[4] grand sea.
Caesar   Be't so, declare thine office.   10
Euphronius Lord of his fortunes he salutes thee, and
  Requires[5] to live in Egypt, which not granted,
  He lessens his requests, and to thee sues
  To let him breathe between the heavens and earth,
  A private man in Athens. This for him.   15
  Next, Cleopatra does confess thy greatness,
  Submits her to thy might, and of thee craves

1 he is plucked = Antony has lost all his feathers ("denuded")
2 feather
3 overabundance
4 to his = compared to the
5 asks

The circle[6] of the Ptolemies for her heirs,
Now hazarded[7] to thy grace.

Caesar   For Antony,

20   I have no ears to his request. The Queen
Of audience nor desire shall fail, so[8] she
From Egypt drive her all-disgracèd friend,
Or take his life there. This if she perform,
She shall not sue unheard. So to them both.

Euphronius Fortune pursue thee!

25   *Caesar*   Bring him through the bands.[9]

EXIT EUPHRONIUS

(*to Thidias*) To try thy eloquence, now 'tis time, dispatch,
From Antony win Cleopatra. Promise,
And in our name, what she requires, add more,
From thine invention[10] – offers.[11] Women are not

30   In[12] their best fortunes strong, but want will perjure[13]
The ne'er-touched vestal.[14] Try thy cunning, Thidias,
Make thine own edict[15] for thy pains,[16] which we
Will answer[17] as a law.

Thidias   Caesar, I go.

6 crown
7 subject
8 if
9 troops
10 contrivance, devising
11 make offers
12 when in
13 want will perjure = deficiency will corrupt
14 sacred virgin
15 make thine own edict = issue your own order/decree
16 trouble (i.e., for his reimbursement/reward)
17 be accountable for/respond to

Caesar Observe how Antony becomes his flaw,[18]
    And what thou think'st his very action speaks[19]   35
    In every power that moves.[20]
Thidias   Caesar, I shall.

EXEUNT

18 becomes his flaw = deals with/adjusts to his failure
19 very action speaks = actual deeds express/signify
20 power that moves = aspect of his behavior

SCENE 13
Alexandria, Cleopatra's palace

ENTER CLEOPATRA, ENOBARBUS, CHARMIAN, AND IRAS

Cleopatra   What shall we[1] do, Enobarbus?

Enobarbus   Think, and die.

Cleopatra   Is Antony or we in fault for this?

Enobarbus   Antony only, that would make his will
　Lord of his reason. What though you fled
5　From that great face[2] of war, whose several ranges[3]
　Frighted each other? Why should he follow?
　The itch of his affection should not then
　Have nicked[4] his captainship, at such a point,
　When half to half the world opposed, he being
10　The merèd[5] question. 'Twas a shame no less
　Than was his loss, to course[6] your flying flags,
　And leave his navy gazing.

Cleopatra   Prithee, peace.[7]

ENTER ANTONY WITH EUPHRONIUS, CAESAR'S AMBASSADOR

Antony   Is that his answer?

Euphronius   Ay, my lord.

15　*Antony*   The Queen shall then have courtesy,[8] so[9] she

1 shall we = must I
2 sight, presence
3 several ranges = different lines/movements
4 cut short
5 sole
6 pursue
7 be silent/quiet*
8 benevolence, consideration, generosity
9 if

Will yield us[10] up.

Euphronius   He says so.

Antony   Let her know't.
  (*to Cleopatra*) To the boy Caesar send this grizzled head,
  And he will fill thy wishes to the brim
  With principalities.[11]

Cleopatra   That head, my lord?

Antony   (*to Euphronius*) To[12] him again, tell him he wears   20
  the rose
  Of youth upon him, from which the world should note
  Something particular.[13] His coin, ships, legions,
  May be a coward's, whose ministers[14] would prevail
  Under the service of a child as soon
  As i' the command of Caesar. I dare him therefore   25
  To lay his gay comparisons apart,[15]
  And answer me, declined,[16] sword against sword,
  Ourselves alone. I'll write it. Follow me.

EXEUNT ANTONY AND EUPHRONIUS

Enobarbus (*aside*) Yes, like enough. High-battled[17] Caesar will
  Unstate[18] his happiness, and be staged to th' show[19]   30

10 me
11 sovereignties
12 go to
13 individually distinctive
14 agents
15 lay his gay comparisons apart = set his brilliant advantages aside
16 (adjective modifying "me") fallen, diminished, deteriorated
17 (?) made great by military success
18 shed
19 staged to th' show = made a public spectacle

Against a sworder![20] I see[21] men's judgments are
A parcel[22] of their fortunes, and things outward
Do draw the inward quality after them,
To suffer all alike. That he should dream,
35   Knowing all measures,[23] the full[24] Caesar will
Answer his emptiness! Caesar, thou hast subdued
His judgment too.

ENTER AN ATTENDANT

Attendant   A messenger from Caesar.
Cleopatra   What, no more ceremony? See, my women,
Against the blown[25] rose may they stop[26] their nose
40   That[27] kneeled unto the buds. Admit him, sir.

EXIT ATTENDANT

Enobarbus (*aside*) Mine honesty and I begin to square.
The loyalty well held to fools does make
Our faith mere folly. Yet he that can endure
To follow with allegiance a fallen lord
45   Does conquer him that did his master conquer
And earns a place i' the story.

ENTER THIDIAS

---

20 (1) master swordsman, (2) gladiator
21 see/understand that
22 of a piece with, an integral portion of
23 (?) *either* (1) as much as he does about fencing, *or* (2) sorts of characters/
    dispositions (from experience)
24 all-powerful★
25 stale
26 hold
27 who

Cleopatra	Caesar's will?
Thidias	Hear it apart.[28]
Cleopatra	None but friends. Say[29] boldly.
Thidias	So haply[30] are they friends to Antony.

Enobarbus He needs as many, sir, as Caesar has,
Or[31] needs not us. If Caesar please, our master   50
Will leap to be his friend. For us you know,
Whose he is, we are,[32] and that is Caesar's.

Thidias   So.
(to Cleopatra) Thus then, thou most renowned. Caesar
  entreats,[33]
Not to consider in what case[34] thou stand'st,
Further than[35] he is Caesar.

Cleopatra   Go on, right royal.[36]   55

Thidias   He knows that you embrace not Antony
As you did love, but as you feared him.

Cleopatra   O!

Thidias   The scars upon your honor, therefore, he
Does pity, as constrainèd blemishes,
Not as deserved.

Cleopatra   He is a god, and knows   60
What is most right. Mine honor was not yielded,

28 privately, aside
29 speak
30 perhaps
31 or else
32 whose he is, we are = whomever Antony owes allegiance to, we owe that
    same allegiance
33 negotiates with you
34 state, circumstance
35 further than = but simply that
36 right royal = Caesar speaks most magnificently

But conquered merely.

Enobarbus   (aside) To be sure of that,
 I will ask Antony. Sir, sir, thou art so leaky
 That we must leave thee to thy sinking, for
 Thy dearest quit thee.

EXIT ENOBARBUS

65 Thidias   Shall I say to Caesar
 What you require of him? For he partly begs
 To be desired to give. It much would please him
 That of his fortunes you should make a staff
 To lean upon. But it would warm his spirits
70 To hear from me you had left Antony,
 And put yourself under his shroud,[37]
 The universal landlord.[38]

Cleopatra   What's your name?

Thidias   My name is Thidias.

Cleopatra   Most kind messenger,
 Say to great Caesar this in disputation,[39]
75 I kiss his conquering hand. Tell him, I am prompt
 To lay my crown at 's[40] feet, and there to kneel.
 Tell him from his all-obeying breath[41] I hear
 The doom of Egypt.[42]

Thidias   'Tis your noblest course.
 Wisdom and fortune combating together,

37 shelter, protection
38 host (as in an inn)
39 in disputation = as a matter of/for discussion
40 at his
41 all-obeying breath = voice that is universally obeyed
42 doom of Egypt = my destiny

If that the former dare but what it can,   80

No chance may shake it. Give me grace to lay

My duty[43] on your hand.

Cleopatra   Your Caesar's father[44] oft,

When he hath mused[45] of taking kingdoms in,

Bestowed his lips on that unworthy place,

As it rained kisses.

ENTER ANTONY AND ENOBARBUS

Antony   Favors?[46] By Jove that thunders!   85

What art thou, fellow?

Thidias   One that but performs

The bidding of the fullest man, and worthiest

To have command obeyed.

Enobarbus   (*aside*) You will be whipped.

Antony   (*to Attendants*) Approach, there! Ah, you kite![47] Now

gods and devils!

Authority melts from me of late. When I cried "Ho,"   90

Like boys unto a muss,[48] kings would start forth,

And cry, "Your will?" Have you no ears? I am

Antony yet.

ENTER ATTENDANTS

Take hence this Jack,[49] and whip him.

---

43 my duty = a respectful kiss

44 again, Julius Caesar had legally adopted his grandnephew, Octavius Caesar

45 contemplated

46 love tokens

47 bird of prey (spoken of Thidias? or of Cleopatra?)

48 a boys' scrambling game: "Ho" would be the signal to begin

49 knave, fellow, rascal

Enobarbus (*aside*) 'Tis better playing with a lion's whelp
  Than with an old one dying.

95 *Antony*   Moon and stars!
  Whip him. Were't twenty of the greatest tributaries[50]
  That do acknowledge Caesar, should I find them
  So saucy[51] with the hand of she here – what's her name,
  Since she was[52] Cleopatra? Whip him fellows,
100 Till like a boy you see him cringe his face,
  And whine aloud for mercy. Take him hence.

Thidias   Mark Antony!

Antony   Tug him away. Being whipped,
  Bring him again. The Jack of Caesar's shall
  Bear us an errand to him.

        EXEUNT ATTENDANTS WITH THIDIAS

105 (*to Cleopatra*) You were half blasted ere I knew you. Ha!
  Have I my pillow left unpressed[53] in Rome,
  Forborne the getting of a lawful race,
  And by a gem of women, to be abused
  By one that looks on feeders?[54]

Cleopatra   Good my lord –

110 *Antony*   You have been a boggler[55] ever,
  But when we in our viciousness grow hard
  (O misery on't!) the wise gods seel[56] our eyes,

50 tribute payers ("vassals")
51 presumptuous★
52 since she was = who used to be
53 unused (not squeezed/pressured)
54 looks on feeders = values servants
55 fence-sitter, opportunist
56 stitch closed (like falcons/hawks being trained)★

In our own filth drop our clear judgments, make us
Adore our errors, laugh at's,[57] while we strut
To our confusion.[58]

Cleopatra   O, is't come to this?   115

Antony   I found you as a morsel cold upon
Dead Caesar's trencher.[59] Nay, you were a fragment[60]
Of Gneius Pompey's,[61] besides what hotter[62] hours,
Unregistered in vulgar fame,[63] you have
Luxuriously[64] picked out. For I am sure,   120
Though you can guess what temperance[65] should be,
You know not what it is.

Cleopatra   Wherefore is this?

Antony   To let a fellow that will take rewards
And say "God quit[66] you" be familiar with
My playfellow, your hand – this kingly seal   125
And plighter[67] of high hearts! O that I were
Upon the hill of Basan,[68] to outroar
The hornèd herd,[69] for I have savage cause,
And to proclaim it civilly,[70] were like

57 at us
58 ruin, destruction
59 platter
60 (i.e., a leftover bit)
61 Pompey the Great, father of the Pompey in this play
62 more ardent
63 unregistered in vulgar fame = unrecorded in common rumor
64 voluptuously, lustfully
65 self-control, restraint, moderation
66 reward
67 seal and plighter = which ratifies/completes and pledges
68 Bashan, ancient Middle Eastern region known for its cattle
69 i.e., Antony too now has horns, as a cuckold/woman-betrayed man
70 politely, courteously

130   A haltered neck which does the hangman thank
       For being yare about him.

       ENTER ATTENDANTS WITH THIDIAS

                          Is he whipped?
Attendant   Soundly, my lord.
Antony   Cried he? And begged a' pardon?
Attendant   He did ask favor.[71]

Antony   (*to Thidias*) If that thy father live, let him repent
135   Thou wast not made his daughter, and be thou sorry
       To follow Caesar in his triumph,[72] since
       Thou hast been whipped for following him. Henceforth
       The[73] white hand of a lady fever thee,
       Shake thou to look on 't. Get thee back to Caesar,
140   Tell him thy entertainment.[74] Look[75] thou say
       He makes me angry with him, for he seems
       Proud and disdainful, harping on what I am,
       Not what he knew I was. He makes me angry;
       And at this time most easy 'tis to do't,
145   When my good stars, that were my former guides,
       Have empty left their orbs,[76] and shot their fires
       Into the abysm of hell. If he mislike
       My speech and what is done, tell him he has
       Hipparchus, my enfranchèd[77] bondman, whom

71 for kindness
72 triumphal procession into Rome★
73 let the
74 reception★
75 be careful that
76 orbits
77 freed

He may at pleasure whip, or hang, or torture,   150
As he shall like, to quit[78] me. Urge it thou.
Hence with thy stripes, be gone!

EXIT THIDIAS

Cleopatra Have you done yet?
Antony   Alack, our terrene moon[79]
  Is now eclipsed, and it portends alone[80]
  The fall of Antony.
Cleopatra   I must stay his time.[81]   155
Antony   To flatter Caesar, would you mingle eyes[82]
  With one that ties his points?[83]
Cleopatra   Not know[84] me yet?
Antony   Cold-hearted toward me?
Cleopatra   Ah, dear, if I be so,
  From my cold heart let heaven engender hail,
  And poison it in the source, and the first stone   160
  Drop in my neck. As it determines,[85] so
  Dissolve my life! The next Caesarion smite![86]
  Till by degrees the memory of my womb,
  Together with my brave Egyptians all,

78 repay
79 terrene moon = earthly ("human") moon goddess, Cleopatra★
80 portends alone = only predicts
81 stay his time = wait/be still/patient until he is ready
82 mingle eyes = associate, be friendly with
83 his points = Caesar's laces (i.e., a servant)
84 recognize
85 melts
86 Caesarion smite = kill the next Caesarion, Cleopatra's son by Julius Caesar
  (see act 3, scene 3, line 6)

165   By the discandying[87] of this pelleted storm[88]
        Lie graveless, till the flies and gnats of Nile
        Have buried them for prey!

    Antony   I am satisfied.
        Caesar sits down in Alexandria, where
        I will oppose his fate.[89] Our force by land
170   Hath nobly held, our severed[90] navy too
        Have knit again, and fleet,[91] threatening most sea-like.
        Where hast thou been, my heart? Dost thou hear, lady?
        If from the field I shall return once more
        To kiss these lips, I will appear in blood,
175   I and my sword will earn our chronicle.
        There's hope in't yet.

    Cleopatra   That's my brave lord!

    Antony   I will be treble-sinewed, -hearted, -breathed,
        And fight maliciously.[92] For when mine hours
        Were nice[93] and lucky, men did ransom lives
180   Of me for jests. But now I'll set my teeth,
        And send to darkness all that stop me. Come,
        Let's have one other gaudy[94] night. Call to me
        All my sad captains, fill our bowls once more.
        Let's mock the midnight bell.

    Cleopatra   It is my birthday,

---

87 melting, dissolving★
88 pelleted storm = hailstorm
89 destiny
90 disunited
91 sail
92 violently
93 wanton, lascivious
94 other gaudy = additional/more luxurious/brilliant

I had thought t' have held it poor.[95] But since my lord   185
Is Antony again, I will be Cleopatra.

Antony   We will yet do well.

Cleopatra   (*to Attendants*) Call all his noble captains to my lord.

Antony   Do so, we'll speak to them, and tonight I'll force
The wine peep[96] through their scars. Come on, my queen,   190
There's sap[97] in't yet. The next time I do fight,
I'll make death love me, for I will contend
Even with his pestilent[98] scythe.

EXEUNT ALL BUT Enobarbus

Enobarbus Now he'll outstare the lightning. To be furious[99]
Is to be frighted out of fear, and in that mood   195
The dove will peck the estridge.[100] And I see still
A diminution in our captain's brain
Restores his heart. When valor preys on reason,
It eats the sword it fights with. I will seek
Some way to leave him.   200

EXIT Enobarbus

95 held it poor = kept/observed it poorly
96 to peer
97 life
98 deadly
99 frantic, raging
100 ostrich

Act 4

Before Alexandria, Caesar's camp

ENTER CAESAR, AGRIPPA, AND MAECENAS, WITH HIS ARMY

Caesar   (*reading a letter*) He calls me boy, and chides, as[1] he had
    power
    To beat me out of Egypt. My messenger
    He hath whipped with rods, dares me to personal combat.
    Caesar to Antony: let the old ruffian[2] know
    I have many other ways to die. Meantime
5   Laugh at his challenge.
Maecenas   Caesar must think,
    When one so great begins to rage, he's hunted
    Even to falling. Give him no breath, but now
    Make boot[3] of his distraction. Never[4] anger
    Made good guard[5] for itself.

---

1 as if
2 cutthroat, bully, swaggerer
3 advantage, profit
4 never did
5 protection, guardian

Caesar   Let our best heads[6]
   Know that tomorrow the last of many battles   10
   We mean to fight.[7] Within our files[8] there are,
   Of those that served Mark Antony but late,
   Enough to fetch him in.[9] See it done,
   And feast the army; we have store to do't,
   And they have earned the waste.[10] Poor Antony!   15

                    EXEUNT

   6 leaders, commanders
   7 i.e., we mean to fight the last of many battles tomorrow
   8 ranks
   9 fetch him in = surround and capture him
  10 extravagance

SCENE 2

Alexandria, Cleopatra's palace

ENTER ANTONY, CLEOPATRA, ENOBARBUS, CHARMIAN,
IRAS, AND ALEXAS, WITH OTHERS

Antony	He will not fight with me, Domitius.
Enobarbus	No.
Antony	Why should he not?

Enobarbus He thinks, being twenty times of better fortune,
He is twenty men to one.

Antony   Tomorrow, soldier,
5   By sea and land I'll fight. Or[1] I will live,
Or bathe[2] my dying honor in the blood
Shall make it live again. Woo't[3] thou fight well?

Enobarbus I'll strike, and cry, "Take all!"[4]

Antony   Well said, come on.
Call forth my household servants, let's tonight
Be bounteous at our meal.

ENTER SERVANTS

10   (*to Servants*) Give me thy hand,
Thou hast been rightly honest. So hast thou,
Thou, and thou, and thou. You have served me well,
And kings have been your fellows.[5]

Cleopatra (*aside to Enobarbus*) What means this?

---

1 either
2 by bathing
3 will you★
4 take all = victory or death
5 i.e., kings have also served me

Enobarbus (*aside to Cleopatra*) 'Tis one of those odd tricks[6]
    which sorrow shoots 15
    Out of the mind.
Antony And thou art honest too.
    I wish I could be made so many men,
    And all of you clapped up[7] together in
    An Antony, that I might do you service
    So good as you have done.
All The gods forbid! 20
Antony Well, my good fellows, wait on me tonight.
    Scant not my cups, and make as much of me
    As when mine empire was your fellow too,
    And suffered my command.
Cleopatra (*aside to Enobabus*) What does he mean? 25
Enobarbus (*aside to Cleopatra*) To make his followers weep.
Antony Tend
    me tonight,
    May be,[8] it is the period[9] of your duty,
    Haply you shall not see me more, or if,
    A mangled shadow. Perchance tomorrow
    You'll serve another master. I look on you 30
    As one that[10] takes his leave. Mine honest friends,
    I turn you not away,[11] but like a master
    Married to your good service, stay till death.
    Tend me tonight two hours, I ask no more,

6 whims, frolics
7 clapped up = placed
8 may be = it may be that
9 end
10 one that = someone who
11 turn you not away = do not dismiss you

And the gods yield[12] you for't!

35 *Enobarbus*   What mean you, sir,
To give them this discomfort? Look, they weep,
And I, an ass, am onion-eyed. For shame,
Transform us not to women.

Antony   Ho, ho, ho!
Now the witch take me,[13] if I meant it thus!
40 Grace grow where those drops fall, my hearty friends,
You take me in too dolorous a sense.
For I spake to you for your comfort, did desire you
To burn[14] this night with torches. Know, my hearts,[15]
I hope well of tomorrow and will lead you
45 Where rather I'll expect victorious life
Than death and honor. Let's to supper, come,
And drown consideration.[16]

EXEUNT

12 repay
13 the witch take me = may I be bewitched
14 light up
15 good fellows
16 contemplation, thought

SCENE 3
Alexandra, before Cleopatra's palace

ENTER TWO SOLDIERS

Soldier 1 Brother, good night. Tomorrow is the day.

Soldier 2 It will determine one way. Fare you well.

   Heard you of nothing strange about the streets?

Soldier 1 Nothing. What news?   5

Soldier 2 Belike 'tis but a rumor. Good night to you.

Soldier 1 Well sir, good night.

ENTER TWO MORE SOLDIERS

Soldier 2 Soldiers, have careful[1] watch.

Soldier 3 And you. Good night, good night.

THEY PLACE THEMSELVES IN EVERY CORNER OF THE STAGE

Soldier 4 Here we.[2] And if tomorrow

   Our navy thrive, I have an absolute hope   10

   Our landmen will stand up.

Soldier 3   'Tis a brave army,

   And full of purpose.[3]

OBOE MUSIC, AS IF UNDER THE STAGE

Soldier 4   Peace, what noise?

Soldier 1   List,[4] list!

Soldier 2 Hark!

Soldier 1   Music i' th' air.

1 attentive
2 here we are ("here is where we are supposed to be")
3 determination, resolution
4 listen★

Soldier 3   Under the earth.

Soldier 4 It signs[5] well, does it not?

Soldier 3   No.

Soldier 1   Peace, I say!

15   What should this mean?

Soldier 2 'Tis the god Hercules, whom Antony loved,
    Now leaves him.

Soldier 1   Walk, let's see if other watchmen
    Do hear what we do.

Soldier 2   How now, masters.[6]

All   (all speaking at once) How now? How now? Do you hear
    this?

Soldier 1 Ay; is't not strange?

Soldier 3   Do you hear, masters? Do you

20   hear?

Soldier 1 Follow the noise so far as we have quarter.[7]
    Let's see how it will give off.[8]

All   Content.[9] 'Tis strange.

EXEUNT

5 betokens, indicates
6 fellows
7 as far as our watch extends (spatially? temporally?)
8 give off = stop
9 agreed

SCENE 4

Alexandria, a room in Cleopatra's palace

ENTER ANTONY, CLEOPATRA, CHARMIAN, AND ATTENDANTS

Antony   Eros, mine armor, Eros!

Cleopatra   Sleep a little.

Antony   No, my chuck. Eros, come, mine armor, Eros!

ENTER EROS WITH ARMOR

Come good fellow, put mine[1] iron on.

If fortune be not ours today, it is

Because we brave[2] her. Come.

Cleopatra   Nay, I'll help too.   5

What's this for?

Antony   Ah, let be, let be! Thou art

The armorer of my heart. False, false.[3] This, this.[4]

Cleopatra Sooth, la, I'll help. Thus it must be.

Antony   Well, well,

We shall thrive now. Seest thou, my good fellow?

Go put on thy defenses.

Eros   Briefly,[5] sir.   10

Cleopatra Is not this buckled well?

Antony   Rarely, rarely:[6]

He that unbuckles this, till we do please

---

1 Folio: thine
2 defy
3 wrong, wrong
4 this way, this way
5 soon, in a minute
6 unusually well, splendidly

To daff't[7] for our repose, shall hear a storm.[8]
Thou fumblest, Eros, and my queen's a squire
15 More tight[9] at this than thou. Dispatch. O love,
That thou couldst see my wars today, and knew'st
The royal occupation, thou shouldst see
A workman in't.

ENTER AN ARMED[10] SOLDIER

Good morrow[11] to thee, welcome,
Thou look'st like him that knows a warlike charge.[12]
20 To business that we love we rise betime,[13]
And go to't with delight.
Soldier   A thousand, sir,
Early though't[14] be, have on their riveted trim,[15]
And at the port[16] expect you.

SHOUT

TRUMPET FLOURISH

ENTER CAPTAINS AND SOLDIERS

Captain The morn is fair. Good morrow, general.
All   Good morrow, general.

---

7 take it off ("doff")
8 violent, protesting outburst
9 able, skillful
10 in armor
11 morning
12 task, responsibility
13 early★
14 though it
15 armor
16 city gates

Antony   'Tis well blown,[17] lads.   25
   This morning, like the spirit of a youth
   That means to be of note,[18] begins betimes.
   So, so. Come give me that, this way, well said.
   Fare thee well, dame, whate'er becomes of me
   This is a soldier's kiss. Rebukeable   30
   (*he kisses her*) And worthy shameful check[19] it were, to stand
   On more mechanic[20] compliment. I'll leave thee
   Now, like a man of steel. You that will fight,
   Follow me close, I'll bring you to't. Adieu.

   EXEUNT ANTONY, EROS, CAPTAINS, AND SOLDIERS

Charmian Please you, retire[21] to your chamber.
Cleopatra   Lead me.   35
   He goes forth gallantly. That[22] he and Caesar might
   Determine this great war in single fight!
   Then Antony – but now – well, on.

EXEUNT

17 the trumpet flourish, just blown
18 distinctive, distinguished
19 evil turn/trick, reproach
20 base, vulgar, common★
21 withdraw★
22 if only

SCENE 5
Alexandria, Antony's camp

TRUMPETS SOUND

ENTER ANTONY AND EROS, A SOLDIER MEETING THEM

Soldier   The gods make this a happy day to Antony!

Antony   Would thou and those thy scars had once[1] prevailed
To make me fight at land.

Soldier   Hadst thou done so,
The kings that have revolted, and the soldier
That has this morning left thee, would have still
Followed thy heels.

Antony   Who's gone this morning?

Soldier   Who?
One ever near thee. Call for Enobarbus,
He shall not hear thee, or from Caesar's camp
Say "I am none of thine."

Antony   What say'st thou?

Soldier   Sir,
He is with Caesar.

Eros   Sir, his chests and treasure
He has not with him.

Antony   Is he gone?

Soldier   Most certain.

Antony   Go Eros, send his treasure after, do it,
Detain no jot,[2] I charge thee. Write to him
(I will subscribe)[3] gentle adieus and greetings,

1 in the first place
2 no jot = not the smallest bit
3 sign my name

Say that I wish he never find more cause   15
To change a master. O my fortunes have
Corrupted honest men. Dispatch. – Enobarbus!

EXEUNT

SCENE 6
Alexandria, Caesar's camp

FLOURISH

ENTER CAESAR, AGRIPPA, WITH ENOBARBUS AND OTHERS

Caesar   Go forth, Agrippa, and begin the fight.
Our will is Antony be took alive.
Make it so known.
Agrippa   Caesar, I shall.

EXIT AGRIPPA

Caesar   The time of universal peace is near.
5   Prove this[1] a prosp'rous day, the three-nooked[2] world
Shall bear[3] the olive freely.[4]

ENTER A MESSENGER

Messenger   Antony
Is come into the field.
Caesar   Go charge Agrippa,
Plant those that have revolted in the van,[5]
That Antony may seem to spend his fury
10   Upon himself.

EXEUNT ALL BUT ENOBARBUS

Enobarbus Alexas did revolt, and went to Jewry[6] on

1 prove this = if this turn out to be
2 three-cornered ("triangular": Europe, Asia, Africa)
3 grow
4 without restraint
5 in the van = foremost ("vanguard")
6 Judea

Affairs of Antony; there did dissuade[7]
Great Herod to incline[8] himself to Caesar,
And leave his master Antony. For this pains
Caesar hath hanged him. Canidius and the rest   15
That fell away have entertainment, but
No honorable trust. I have done ill,
Of which I do accuse myself so sorely
That I will joy no more.

ENTER A SOLDIER OF CAESAR'S

Soldier   Enobarbus, Antony
Hath after thee sent all thy treasure, with   20
His bounty overplus.[9] The messenger
Came on my guard,[10] and at thy tent is now
Unloading of his mules.
Enobarbus   I give it you.
Soldier   Mock not, Enobarbus,
I tell you true. Best you safed[11] the bringer   25
Out of the host,[12] I must attend mine office
Or would have done't myself. Your emperor
Continues still a Jove.[13]

EXIT SOLDIER

Enobarbus I am alone the villain[14] of the earth,

7 advise, persuade
8 subject (verb)
9 bounty overplus = a gift/generosity★ in addition
10 watch
11 gave a safe-conduct to
12 out of the host = so he can go back through the army's lines
13 i.e., to act like a supreme ruler
14 alone the villain = the only villain

30   And feel I am so most.[15] O Antony,
        Thou mine of bounty,[16] how wouldst thou have paid
        My better service, when my turpitude[17]
        Thou dost so crown with gold! This blows[18] my heart,
        If swift thought[19] break it not. A swifter mean[20]
35   Shall outstrike[21] thought, but thought will do't, I feel.
        I fight against thee?[22] No, I will go seek
        Some ditch wherein to die. The foul'st best fits
        My latter[23] part of life.

EXIT ENOBARBUS

15 feel I am so most = feel most that I am so
16 generosity
17 baseness, depravity
18 shatters, explodes
19 (1) mental activity in general, (2) anxiety
20 means, measure, course
21 hit harder than
22 Antony
23 concluding

SCENE 7
Battlefield between the camps

ALARUM

DRUMS AND TRUMPETS

ENTER AGRIPPA AND OTHERS

Agrippa Retire, we have engaged ourselves too far.
　Caesar himself has[1] work, and our oppression[2]
　Exceeds what we expected.

EXEUNT

ALARUMS

ENTER ANTONY, AND SCARUS WOUNDED

Scarus　O my brave emperor, this is fought indeed!
　Had we done so at first,[3] we had droven them home　　　　5
　With clouts[4] about their heads.
Antony　　　　　　　　　　Thou bleed'st apace.
Scarus　I had a wound here that was like a T,
　But now 'tis made an H.[5]
Antony　　　　　　　　They do retire.
Scarus　We'll beat 'em into bench-holes,[6] I have yet
　Room for six scotches[7] more.　　　　　　　　　　　　　10

1 will be required to
2 difficulty, trouble
3 i.e., instead of fighting at sea
4 rags, bandages
5 i.e., it has an extra line, is larger
6 privies, toilets
7 cuts, gashes

ENTER EROS

Eros   They are beaten sir, and our advantage serves[8]
        For a fair victory.

Scarus   Let us score[9] their backs,
        And snatch 'em up, as we take hares, behind.[10]
        'Tis sport to maul[11] a runner.

Antony   I will reward thee
15   Once for thy spritely[12] comfort, and tenfold
        For thy good valor. Come thee on.

Scarus   I'll halt[13] after.

EXEUNT

  8 is worthy of, earns
  9 mark, whip, cut
 10 from behind
 11 hammer, beat
 12 spirited, lively
 13 limp

SCENE 8
Under the walls of Alexandria

ALARUM

ENTER ANTONY, MARCHING, SCARUS, AND OTHERS

Antony We have beat him[1] to his camp. Run one before,
　　And let the Queen know of our gests.[2] Tomorrow,
　　Before the sun shall see 's, we'll spill the blood
　　That has today escaped. I thank you all,
　　For doughty-handed[3] are you, and have fought   5
　　Not as you served the cause, but as 't[4] had been
　　Each man's like mine. You have shown[5] all Hectors.[6]
　　Enter the city, clip[7] your wives, your friends,
　　Tell them your feats, whilst they with joyful tears
　　Wash the congealment[8] from your wounds, and kiss   10
　　The honored gashes whole.[9] *(to Scarus)* Give me thy hand

ENTER CLEOPATRA, WITH ATTENDANTS

　　To this great fairy[10] I'll commend thy acts,
　　Make her thanks bless thee. *(to Cleopatra)* O thou day o' the
　　world,

1 beat him = beaten him back
2 exploits, notable deeds
3 valiant, brave, formidable
4 as if it = as if the cause
5 shown yourselves to be
6 Trojan prince and chief defender of Troy
7 embrace
8 clotted blood
9 i.e., make the gashes whole by kissing them
10 enchantress

Chain[11] mine armed neck, leap thou, attire and all,

15   Through proof of harness[12] to my heart, and there

Ride on the pants,[13] triumphing!

Cleopatra   Lord of lords,

O infinite virtue,[14] comest thou smiling from

The world's great snare[15] uncaught?

Antony   My nightingale,

We have beat them to their beds. What girl, though gray

20   Do something mingle with our[16] younger brown, yet ha' we

A brain that nourishes our nerves,[17] and can

Get goal for goal of youth.[18] Behold this man,[19]

Commend[20] unto his lips thy favoring[21] hand.

(*to Scarus*) Kiss it, my warrior. (*to Cleopatra*) He hath fought today

25   As if a god, in hate of mankind, had

Destroyed in[22] such a shape.

Cleopatra   (*to Scarus*) I'll give thee, friend,

An armor all of gold. It was a king's.

Antony   He has deserved it, were it carbuncled[23]

Like holy Phoebus' car.[24] Give me thy hand.

---

11 embrace
12 proof of harness = tested armor/equipment
13 quick breaths
14 power, excellence
15 trap
16 my
17 sinews, muscles
18 i.e., compete on equal terms with younger people
19 Scarus
20 entrust, commit
21 approving, indulgent
22 by using
23 covered with sapphires and rubies
24 chariot

Through Alexandria make a jolly march,   30
Bear our hacked[25] targets like the men that owe[26] them.
Had our great palace the capacity
To camp[27] this host, we all would sup together,
And drink carouses to the next day's fate,
Which promises royal[28] peril. Trumpeters,   35
With brazen[29] din blast you the city's ear,
Make mingle with rattling taborines,[30]
That heaven and earth may strike their sounds together,
Applauding our approach.

EXEUNT

25 mangled, slashed
26 own
27 lodge (verb)
28 promises royal = makes us expect magnificent/splendid
29 brassy
30 rattling taborines = rapid/lively drums

SCENE 9
Caesar's camp

SENTINELS AT THEIR POST

Soldier 1   If we be not relieved within this hour,
We must return to th' court of guard.[1] The night
Is shiny,[2] and they say we shall embattle[3]
By th' second hour i' the morn.
Soldier 2   This last day was
A shrewd[4] one to's.[5]

ENTER ENOBARBUS

5 *Enobarbus*   O bear me witness, night –
Soldier 3   What man is this?
Soldier 2   Stand close, and list him.
Enobarbus Be witness to me (O thou blessèd moon),
When men revolted[6] shall upon record[7]
Bear hateful memory. Poor Enobarbus did
Before thy face repent.
Soldier 1   Enobarbus?
10 *Soldier 3*   Peace.
Hark further.
Enobarbus O sovereign mistress[8] of true melancholy,

---

1 court of guard = *corps de garde,* guardhouse
2 bright, luminous
3 take to the battlefield
4 fierce, harmful
5 to/for us
6 rebellious, insurgent
7 written evidence
8 the moon

The poisonous damp of night disponge[9] upon me,
That life, a very rebel to my will,
May hang no longer on me. Throw my heart   15
Against the flint and hardness of my fault,
Which being dried with grief, will break to powder,
And finish all foul thoughts. O Antony,
Nobler[10] than my revolt is infamous,[11]
Forgive me in thine own particular,[12]   20
But let the world rank me in register[13]
A master-leaver[14] and a fugitive.
O Antony! O Antony!

ENOBARBUS DIES

Soldier 2   Let's speak to him.
Soldier 1 Let's hear him, for the things he speaks
    May concern Caesar.
Soldier 3   Let's do so. But he sleeps.   25
Soldier 1 Swoons rather, for so bad a prayer as his
    Was never yet for[15] sleep.
Soldier 2   Go we to him.
Soldier 3 Awake sir, awake, speak to us.
Soldier 2   Hear you, sir?
Soldier 1 The hand of death hath raught[16] him.

 9 pour down
10 you who are more noble
11 evil
12 in thine own particular = as an individual, you yourself
13 its lists/books of record
14 one who abandons his master
15 made in preparation for, just before
16 reached, snatched at

DRUMS FAR OFF

30   Hark, the drums demurely[17] wake the sleepers.
      Let us bear him to the court of guard.
      He is of note.[18] Our hour[19] is fully out.[20]
      Soldier 3 Come on then, he may recover yet.

EXEUNT WITH THE BODY

17 gravely, quietly
18 of note = an eminent/notable person
19 stated time of duty
20 over

SCENE 10

Between the two camps

ENTER ANTONY AND SCARUS, WITH THEIR ARMY

Antony Their preparation is today by sea,
We please them not by land.
Scarus   For both,[1] my lord.
Antony I would they'ld fight i' th' fire or i' th' air,
We'ld fight there too. But this it is, our foot[2]
Upon the hills adjoining to the city   5
Shall stay with us. Order for sea is[3] given,
They[4] have put forth the haven.[5]
Where their appointment[6] we may best[7] discover,
And look on their endeavor.[8]

EXEUNT

1 i.e., we displease them both at sea and on land
2 foot soldiers, infantry
3 has been
4 Caesar's ships
5 put forth the haven = left the harbor
6 direction, destination
7 for the best, to the extent possible
8 enterprise

SCENE 11

A place between the two camps

ENTER CAESAR AND HIS ARMY

Caesar But[1] being charged,[2] we will be still by land,
　　Which as I take't we shall, for his best force[3]
　　Is forth[4] to man his galleys. To the vales,[5]
　　And hold[6] our best advantage.[7]

EXEUNT

1 except in the event that
2 attacked
3 strength, might, power
4 has been actively engaged/committed
5 ground between hills
6 procure, get, take
7 position

SCENE 12

A place between the two camps

Antony Yet they are not joined.[1] Where yond pine does stand,
　　I shall discover all. I'll bring thee word
　　Straight, how 'tis like to go.

Scarus　　　　　　　　　　Swallows have built
　　In Cleopatra's sails their nests. The augurers[2]
　　Say they know not, they cannot tell, look grimly,[3]　　　　5
　　And dare not speak their knowledge. Antony
　　Is valiant, and dejected, and by starts
　　His fretted[4] fortunes give him hope and fear
　　Of what he has, and has not.

Antony　　　　　　　　　　All is lost.
　　This foul Egyptian hath betrayed me.　　　　　　　　　10
　　My fleet hath yielded to the foe, and yonder
　　They cast their caps up and carouse together
　　Like friends long lost. Triple-turned[5] whore! 'Tis thou
　　Hast sold me to this novice, and my heart
　　Makes only wars on thee. Bid them all fly,　　　　　　15

---

1 they are not joined = the two naval forces have not begun to fight
2 predictors of the future (Folio: auguries)★
3 (1) awful, terrible, (2) afraid
4 worn-out, distressed
5 three times turned

For when I am revenged upon my charm,[6]
I have done all. Bid them all fly, be gone.

EXIT SCARUS

O sun, thy uprise shall I see no more.
Fortune and Antony part here, even here
20   Do we shake hands. All come to this? The hearts
That spanieled me[7] at heels, to whom I gave
Their wishes, do discandy, melt their sweets
On blossoming Caesar. And this pine[8] is barked,[9]
That overtopped them all. Betrayed I am.
25   O this false soul of Egypt! This grave charm,
Whose eye becked forth my wars, and called them home,
Whose bosom was my crownet,[10] my chief end,
Like a right[11] gipsy hath, at fast and loose,[12]
Beguiled me to the very heart of loss.
What, Eros, Eros!

ENTER CLEOPATRA

30   Ah, thou spell! Avaunt.[13]
Cleopatra Why is my lord enraged against his love?
Antony   Vanish, or I shall give thee thy deserving,
And blemish Caesar's triumph. Let him take thee,
And hoist thee up to the shouting plebeians,

6 magic spell, bewitching
7 spanieled me = fawned upon me
8 Antony himself
9 stripped of its bark
10 coronet, crown★
11 true
12 a cheating game
13 be gone

Follow his chariot, like the greatest spot[14]   35
Of all thy sex. Most monster-like, be shown
For poor'st diminutives, for dolts, and let
Patient Octavia plough thy visage up
With her preparèd nails.

EXIT CLEOPATRA

           'Tis well thou'rt gone,
If it be well to live. But better 'twere   40
Thou fell'st into my fury, for one death
Might have prevented many. Eros, ho!
The shirt of Nessus[15] is upon me. Teach me,
Alcides,[16] thou mine ancestor, thy rage.
Let me lodge Lichas[17] on the horns o' the moon,   45
And with those hands, that grasped the heaviest club,
Subdue my worthiest self. The witch shall die,
To the young Roman boy she hath sold me, and I fall
Under this plot. She dies for't. Eros, ho!

EXIT

14 blemish, disgrace
15 poisonous shirt that killed Hercules (Herakles)
16 Hercules (alSEEdeez)
17 Hercules' servant (LIEkass), bringer of the poisoned shirt, thrown to the
    moon by Hercules in his agony

SCENE 13

Alexandria, Cleopatra's palace

ENTER CLEOPATRA, CHARMIAN, IRAS, AND MARDIAN

Cleopatra Help me, my women! O he's more mad
    Than Telamon[1] for his shield.[2] The boar of Thessaly[3]
    Was never so embossed.[4]

Charmian   To th' monument![5]
    There lock yourself, and send him word you are dead.

5   The soul and body rive[6] not more in parting
    Than greatness going off.[7]

Cleopatra   To the monument!
    Mardian, go tell him I have slain myself.
    Say that the last I spoke was "Antony,"
    And word it (prithee) piteously. Hence, Mardian,

10   And bring me how he takes my death.
    To the monument!

EXEUNT

---

1 Ajax
2 Ajax wore an all-enveloping body armor, from Mycaenae; the reference here
  may be to the dead Achilles' shield, which Ajax wanted and did not get
3 wild boar sent by Artemis (Diana), in revenge for neglectful worship
4 driven, pursued
5 her tomb
6 are lacerated, torn apart
7 going off = failing (i.e., Antony's upset is caused by his failure)

SCENE 14
Alexandria, a room in Cleopatra's palace

ENTER ANTONY AND EROS

Antony Eros, thou yet behold'st me?

Eros   Ay, noble lord.

Antony Sometime we see a cloud that's dragonish,
A vapor sometime like a bear or lion,
A towered citadel,[1] a pendent rock,
A forkèd mountain, or blue promontory   5
With trees upon't, that nod unto the world,
And mock our eyes with air. Thou hast seen these signs,
They are black vesper's pageants.[2]

Eros   Ay my lord.

Antony That which is now a horse, even with a thought
The rack dislimns,[3] and makes it indistinct,   10
As water is in water.[4]

Eros   It does, my lord.

Antony My good knave Eros, now thy captain is
Even such a body. Here I am Antony,
Yet cannot hold this visible shape, my knave.
I made these wars for Egypt,[5] and the Queen –   15
Whose heart I thought I had, for she had mine,

---

1 fortress, protecting a city
2 black vesper's pageants = scenic representations seen, but only imperfectly, at
  night
3 cloud obliterates
4 as water is in water = as water is when collected in some larger body, sea, lake,
  and so on
5 Cleopatra

Which whilst it was mine had annexed[6] unto't
A million more, now lost – she, Eros, has
Packed cards[7] with Caesar, and false-played my glory
20   Unto an enemy's triumph.
Nay, weep not gentle Eros, there is left us
Ourselves to end ourselves.

ENTER MARDIAN

             O thy vile lady,
She has robbed me of my sword.

Mardian   No Antony,
My mistress loved thee, and her fortunes mingled
With thine entirely.

25 *Antony*   Hence, saucy eunuch, peace!
She hath betrayed me, and shall die the death.[8]

Mardian   Death of one person can be paid but once,
And that she has discharged. What thou wouldst do
Is done unto[9] thy hand. The last she spake
30   Was "Antony! most noble Antony!"
Then in the midst a tearing groan did break
The name of Antony. It was divided
Between her heart and lips. She rendered[10] life
Thy name so[11] buried in her.

Antony   Dead, then?

Mardian   Dead.

---

6 added, joined
7 packed cards = made a cheating arrangement
8 i.e., the death that a traitor/betrayer deserves
9 done unto = performed/executed for
10 gave/returned to
11 thus

Antony Unarm[12] Eros, the long day's task is done,   35
  And we must sleep. (*to Mardian*) That thou depart'st hence safe
  Does pay thy labor richly.[13] Go.

EXIT MARDIAN

                              Off, pluck off.
The sevenfold shield of Ajax[14] cannot keep
The battery[15] from my heart. O cleave, my sides!
Heart, once[16] be stronger than thy continent,[17]   40
Crack thy frail case! Apace, Eros, apace.[18]
No[19] more a soldier. Bruised pieces,[20] go,
You have been nobly borne. (*to Eros*) From[21] me awhile.

EXIT EROS

I will o'ertake thee, Cleopatra,
And weep for my pardon. So it must be, for now   45
All length[22] is torture. Since the torch[23] is out,
Lie down and stray[24] no farther. Now all labor

---

12 (1) take off armor, (2) put away weapons
13 i.e., Antony does not feel obliged to pay him in any way other than via a safe
   conduct back
14 see act 4, scene 13, n.19
15 bruising, beating
16 for once
17 container
18 i.e., get my armor off more quickly
19 I am no
20 bruised pieces = battered parts/fragments (of the entire man/soldier who
   no longer exists)
21 go from
22 (1) time, (2) length of life
23 (1) life, *and* (2) love
24 wander, roam

Mars what it does. Yea, very force entangles[25]
Itself with strength. Seal[26] then and all is done.

50 Eros! – I come, my queen – Eros! – Stay[27] for me.
Where souls do couch[28] on flowers, we'll[29] hand in hand,
And with our sprightly port[30] make the ghosts gaze.
Dido and her Aeneas shall want troops,[31]
And all the haunt[32] be ours. Come Eros! Eros!

ENTER EROS

Eros   What would my lord?
55 *Antony*   Since Cleopatra died,[33]
I have lived in such dishonor, that the gods
Detest my baseness. I, that with my sword
Quartered[34] the world, and o'er green Neptune's back
With ships made cities, condemn[35] myself to lack
60 The courage of a woman, less[36] noble mind
Than she which by her death our Caesar tells
"I am conqueror of myself." Thou art sworn, Eros,
That when the exigent[37] should come – which now
Is come indeed – when I should see behind me

25 very force entangles = force itself is caught/held fast
26 (1) complete, (2) put a seal of finality (as on a document), (3) close up, finish
27 wait
28 lie
29 we will go
30 sprightly port = cheerful/gay manner/bearing
31 want troops = lack followers
32 society, companionship
33 since Cleopatra died = now that Cleopatra is dead
34 divided/cut up
35 censure, convict
36 to have a less
37 critical need/necessity

The inevitable prosecution[38] of   65
Disgrace and horror, that on my command
Thou then wouldst kill me. Do't, the time is come.
Thou strikest not me, 'tis Caesar thou defeat'st.
Put color in thy cheek.

Eros   The gods withhold me!
Shall I do that which all the Parthian darts   70
(Though enemy)[39] lost aim, and could not?

Antony   Eros,
Wouldst thou be windowed[40] in great Rome and see
Thy master thus with pleached[41] arms, bending down[42]
His corrigible[43] neck, his face subdued
To penetrative[44] shame, whilst the wheeled seat[45]   75
Of fortunate Caesar, drawn before him, branded[46]
His baseness that ensued?[47]

Eros   I would not[48] see't.

Antony Come then. For with a wound I must be cured.
Draw that thy honest sword,[49] which thou hast worn
Most useful[50] for thy country.

38 progression, continuation
39 hostile
40 placed at a window
41 tangled, twisted (bound?)
42 thy MASter THUS with PLEACH'D arms BENDing DOWN
43 submissive (CAHRiJIBel)
44 piercing
45 i.e., in a triumphal chariot
46 signaled/marked most ignominiously
47 that ensued = he who followed (Antony, a prisoner bound, trailing behind
   Caesar)
48 would not = do not wish to
49 that thy honest sword = that honest sword of yours
50 advantageously, profitably

80 *Eros*   O sir, pardon[51] me!

Antony When I did make thee free, sworest thou not then

    To do this when I bade thee? Do it at once,

    Or thy precedent[52] services are all

    But[53] accidents unpurposed. Draw, and come.

85 *Eros*   Turn from me, then, that noble countenance,

    Wherein the worship of the whole world lies.

Antony (*turning away his face*) Lo thee![54]

Eros   My sword is drawn.

Antony   Then let it do at once

    The thing why[55] thou hast drawn it.

Eros   My dear master,

90   My captain, and my emperor, let me say,

    Before I strike this bloody stroke, farewell.

Antony 'Tis said, man, and farewell.

Eros   Farewell, great chief. Shall I strike now?

Antony   Now Eros.

Eros   (*killing himself*) Why there then. Thus I do escape the

    sorrow

    Of Antony's death.

95 *Antony*   Thrice-nobler than myself,

    Thou teachest me, O valiant Eros, what

    I should, and thou couldst not. My queen and Eros

    Have by their brave instruction got upon[56] me

    A nobleness in record. But I will be

---

51 excuse
52 previous
53 all but = virtually, almost
54 lo thee = all right, see
55 for which ("the reason why")
56 got upon = earned from / ahead of

A bridegroom in my death, and run into't   100
As to a lover's bed. Come then – and Eros,
Thy master dies thy scholar. To do thus
(*falls on his sword*) I learned of thee. How, not dead? Not
dead?
The guard, ho! O dispatch me!

ENTER DECRETAS[57] AND GUARDSMEN

Guard 1   What's the noise?
Antony   I have done my work ill, friends. O make an end   105
Of what I have begun.
Guard 2   The star is fall'n.
Guard 2   And time is at his period.[58]
All   Alas, and woe.
Antony   Let him that loves me strike me dead.
Guard 1   Not I.
Guard 2   Nor I.
Guard 3   Nor any one.

EXEUNT GUARDSMEN

Decretas   Thy death and fortunes bid thy followers fly.   110
This sword but shown to Caesar, with this tidings,
Shall enter[59] me with him.

ENTER DIOMEDES [60]

Diomedes Where's Antony?

57 dekRAYtus
58 end
59 begin, admit
60 dieOMiDEEZ

Decretas   There Diomed, there.
Diomedes   Lives he?
    (*to Decretas*) Wilt thou not answer, man?

EXIT DECRETAS

115 *Antony*   Art thou there, Diomed? Draw thy sword, and give me
        Sufficing strokes for death.
    Diomedes   Most absolute lord,
        My mistress Cleopatra sent me to thee.
    Antony   When did she send thee?
    Diomedes   Now,[61] my lord.
    Antony   Where is
        she?
    Diomedes Locked in her monument. She had a prophesying fear
120   Of what hath come to pass. For when she saw –
        Which never shall be found – you did suspect
        She had disposed[62] with Caesar, and that your rage
        Would not be purged, she sent you word she was dead.
        But fearing since how it might work, hath sent
125   Me to proclaim the truth, and I am come,
        I dread, too late.
    Antony   Too late good Diomed. Call my guard, I prithee.
    Diomedes What ho, the Emperor's guard! The guard, what ho!
        Come, your lord calls!

ENTER GUARDSMEN

130 *Antony*   Bear me, good friends, where Cleopatra bides,
        'Tis the last service that I shall command you.

61 just now
62 made arrangements

Guard 1 Woe, woe are we sir, you may not live to wear
     All your true followers out.
All   Most heavy day!
Antony Nay, good my fellows, do not please sharp[63] fate
     To grace[64] it with your sorrows. Bid that welcome[65]   135
     Which comes to punish us, and we punish it
     Seeming to bear it lightly. Take me up,
     I have led you oft, carry me now, good friends,
     And have my thanks for all.

                    EXEUNT, BEARING ANTONY

63 keenly piercing
64 by gracing
65 bid that welcome = bid welcome to that

SCENE 15
Cleopatra's monument

ENTER, ALOFT, CLEOPATRA, AND HER MAIDS,
WITH CHARMIAN AND IRAS

Cleopatra O Charmian, I will never go from hence.
Charmian Be comforted, dear madam.
Cleopatra   No, I will not.
  All strange and terrible events are welcome,
  But comforts we despise. Our size[1] of sorrow,
5 Proportioned to our cause, must be as great
  As that which makes it.

ENTER, BELOW, DIOMEDES

                          How now? Is he dead?
Diomedes His death's upon him, but not dead.
  Look out o' the other side your monument,
  His guard have brought him thither.

ENTER, BELOW, ANTONY, BORNE BY GUARDSMEN

Cleopatra   O sun,
10 Burn the great sphere thou movest in,[2] darkling stand[3]
  The varying shore[4] o' the world. O Antony,
  Antony, Antony! Help Charmian, help Iras, help!
  Help, friends below, let's draw him hither.
Antony   Peace!

1 quantity
2 in Ptolemaic astronomy all heavenly bodies were contained in spheres; only
  the spheres moved
3 darkling stand = in darkness remain
4 varying shore = land that is variegating/changing color

Not Caesar's valor hath o'erthrown Antony,
But Antony's hath triumph'd on itself.   15

Cleopatra So it should be, that none but Antony
Should conquer Antony; but woe 'tis so.

Antony   I am dying, Egypt, dying. Only
I here importune[5] death awhile, until
Of many thousand kisses the poor last   20
I lay upon thy lips.

Cleopatra   I dare not,[6] dear,
Dear my lord, pardon. I dare not,
Lest I be taken. Not the imperious show
Of the full-fortuned Caesar ever shall
Be brooched[7] with me, if knife, drugs, serpents, have[8]   25
Edge, sting, or operation.[9] I am safe.[10]
Your wife Octavia, with her modest eyes
And still conclusion,[11] shall acquire no honor[12]
Demuring[13] upon me. But come, come, Antony,
Help me my women, we must draw thee up.   30
Assist, good friends.

Antony   O quick, or I am gone.

Cleopatra Here's sport[14] indeed! How heavy weighs my lord!

5 solicit, petition
6 i.e., do not dare come down to where you are
7 adorned
8 be BROOCHED with ME if KNIVES drugs SERpents HAVE
9 force, performance
10 i.e., safe up here (edge STING or OperAshun I am SAFE)
11 silent (1) demeanor, (2) passing of judgment
12 and STILL conCLEWzeeOWN shall aKWIRE no HONor
13 looking with affected modesty
14 recreation, entertainment

Our strength is all gone into heaviness,[15]
That makes the weight. Had I great Juno's[16] power,
35 The strong-winged Mercury[17] should fetch thee up,
And set thee by Jove's side. Yet come a little,
Wishers were ever fools. O come, come, come,

ANTONY IS BORNE ALOFT

And welcome, welcome! Die when[18] thou hast lived,
Quicken[19] with kissing. Had my lips that power,
Thus would I wear them out.

40 *All*   A heavy sight!
Antony   I am dying, Egypt, dying.
Give me some wine, and let me speak a little.
Cleopatra No, let me speak, and let me rail so high,[20]
That the false huswife[21] Fortune break[22] her wheel,[23]
Provoked[24] by my offense.[25]
45 *Antony*   One word, sweet queen.
Of[26] Caesar seek your honor, with your safety. O!
Cleopatra They[27] do not go together.
Antony   Gentle, hear me,

15 sorrow (with a pun on "heavy weight")
16 wife of Jove, king of the gods
17 winged messenger of the gods
18 after
19 be revived
20 curse/scold so strongly
21 worthless woman/housewife
22 may break
23 spinning wheel
24 being made so angry
25 assault, attack
26 from
27 her honor and her safety

None about Caesar trust[28] but Proculeius.

Cleopatra My resolution,[29] and my hands, I'll trust,
None[30] about Caesar.   50

Antony   The miserable change now at my end[31]
Lament nor sorrow at. But please your thoughts
In feeding them with those my former fortunes
Wherein I lived. The greatest prince o' the world,
The noblest. And do now not basely die,[32]   55
Not cowardly put off[33] my helmet to
My countryman. A Roman by a Roman
Valiantly vanquished. Now my spirit is going,
I can no more.

Cleopatra   Noblest of men, woo't die?
Hast thou no care[34] of me? Shall I abide   60
In this dull world, which in thy absence is
No better than a sty?[35] O see, my women.

ANTONY DIES

The crown o' the earth doth melt. My lord!
O withered is the garland[36] of the war,
The soldier's pole[37] is fall'n. Young boys and girls   65

28 none about Caesar trust = trust no one in Caesar's entourage except
   Proculeius (proCUEleeUS)
29 confidence, positive knowledge, determination*
30 but no one
31 the MizeRAble CHANGE now AT my END
32 the NOblest AND do NOW not BASEly DIE
33 put off = take off (i.e., as an act signifying surrender)
34 concern, anxiety, worry
35 pigsty
36 wreath of flowers, worn like a crown
37 polestar, lodestar, governing principle/standard

Are level[38] now with men. The odds[39] is gone,
And there is nothing left remarkable[40]
Beneath the visiting moon.

CLEOPATRA FAINTS

Charmian	O quietness,[41] lady!
Iras	She is dead too, our sovereign.
Charmian	Lady!
Iras	Madam!
Charmian	O madam, madam, madam!
Iras	Royal Egypt, Empress!
Charmian	Peace, peace, Iras!

Cleopatra No more but e'en[42] a woman, and commanded
By such poor passion as the maid that milks
And does the meanest chares.[43] It were for me
To throw my scepter at the injurious[44] gods,
To tell them that this world did equal theirs
Till they had stol'n our jewel. All's but naught.
Patience is sottish,[45] and impatience does
Become[46] a dog that's mad. Then is it sin
To rush into the secret house of death,
Ere death dare come to us? How do you, women?
What, what, good cheer! Why how now, Charmian?

38 equal
39 differences/distinctions between and among things
40 worth seeing
41 my silent/unmoving one
42 even, just
43 chores★
44 hurtful, harmful
45 stupid
46 turn into?

My noble girls! Ah women, women! Look,
Our lamp is spent, it's out! (*to those below*) Good sirs, take
heart,
We'll bury him. And then, what's brave, what's noble,   85
Let's do it after the high Roman fashion,
And make death proud to take us. Come, away,
This case[47] of that huge spirit now is cold.
Ah women, women! Come, we have no friend
But resolution, and the briefest end.   90

  EXEUNT, THOSE ABOVE BEARING OFF ANTONY'S BODY

47 container, body

Act 5

SCENE I
Alexandria, Caesar's camp

ENTER CAESAR, AGRIPPA, DOLABELLA, MAECENAS,
GALLUS, PROCULEIUS, AND OTHERS, HIS COUNCIL OF WAR

Caesar   Go to him Dolabella, bid him yield.
Being so frustrate, tell him he mocks
The pauses that he makes.

Dolabella   Caesar, I shall.

EXIT DOLABELLA

ENTER DECRETAS, WITH ANTONY'S SWORD

Caesar   Wherefore is that?[1] And what art thou that darest
Appear thus to us?[2]

5   *Decretas*   I am called Decretas,
Mark Antony I served, who best was worthy
Best to be served.[3] Whilst he stood up and spoke,

---

1 wherefore is that = why are you displaying that sword?
2 thus to us = with a bared, blood-stained sword in your hand, to me
3 he was the best person to serve and to serve as best as possible

174

He was my master, and I wore[4] my life
To spend upon his haters. If thou please
To take me to thee, as I was to him   10
I'll be to Caesar. If thou pleasest not,
I yield thee up my life.

Caesar   What is't thou say'st?

Decretas I say, O Caesar, Antony is dead.

Caesar The breaking of so great a thing should make
A greater crack.[5] The round world   15
Should have shook lions into civil streets,
And citizens to their dens. The death of Antony
Is not a single doom,[6] in the name lay
A moiety[7] of the world.

Decretas   He is dead, Caesar,
Not by a public minister of justice,   20
Nor by a hired knife, but that self-hand[8]
Which writ his honor in the acts it did,
Hath with the courage which the heart did lend it,
Splitted the heart. This is his sword,
I robbed his wound of it. Behold it stained   25
With his most noble blood.

Caesar   Look you sad friends,
The[9] gods rebuke me, but it is tidings
To wash the eyes of kings.

Agrippa   And strange it is,

4 employed
5 loud sound, as in thunder or the final judgment of the world ("Doomsday")
6 death, fate
7 (1) half, (2) portion, part (MOYehTEE)
8 same hand
9 may the

That nature must compel us to lament
Our most persisted[10] deeds.

30 *Maecenas*   His taints[11] and honors
Waged[12] equal with him.

Agrippa   A rarer spirit never
Did steer humanity. But you gods will give us
Some faults to make us men. (*Caesar weeps*) Caesar is touched.

Maecenas When such a spacious[13] mirror's set before him,
He needs must see himself.

35 *Caesar*   O Antony!
I have followed[14] thee to this, but we do launch[15]
Diseases in our bodies. I must perforce
Have shown[16] to thee such a declining[17] day,
Or look on thine. We could not stall[18] together,
40 In[19] the whole world. But yet let me lament,
With tears as sovereign as the blood of hearts,
That thou, my brother, my competitor
In top of all design,[20] my mate in empire,
Friend and companion in the front[21] of war,
45 The arm of mine own body, and the heart
Where mine his thoughts did kindle – that our stars,

10 insisted upon, persisted in
11 blemishes, stains, dishonors
12 fought
13 large, ample
14 hunted, pursued
15 shoot
16 displayed, exhibited
17 sinking, setting
18 dwell
19 not in
20 top of all design = highest of all plans/schemes/purposes
21 foremost lines

Unreconciliable, should divide[22]
Our equalness to this. Hear me, good friends –
But I will tell you at some meeter season.

ENTER AN EGYPTIAN

The business[23] of this man looks out of him,   50
We'll hear him what he says. Whence are you?
Egyptian A poor Egyptian yet. The Queen my mistress,
    Confined in all she has, her[24] monument,
    Of thy intents desires instruction,[25]
    That she preparedly[26] may frame[27] herself   55
    To the way she's forced to.
Caesar   Bid her have good heart,
    She soon shall know of us, by some of ours,
    How honorable and how kindly we
    Determine for her, for Caesar cannot leave[28]
    To be ungentle.
Egyptian   So[29] the gods preserve thee!   60

EXIT EGYPTIAN

Caesar   Come hither, Proculeius. Go and say
    We purpose her no shame. Give her what comforts
    The quality of her passion shall require,
    Lest in her greatness, by some mortal stroke

22 break, split, cut asunder
23 purpose, errand
24 which is her
25 knowledge
26 in a state of readiness
27 compose, shape
28 change himself
29 thus may

65   She do defeat us. For her life[30] in Rome
        Would be eternal in our triumph.[31] Go,
        And with your speediest bring us what she says,
        And how you find of her.

Proculeius   Caesar, I shall.

EXIT PROCULEIUS

Caesar   Gallus, go you along.

EXIT GALLUS

70   Where's Dolabella,
        To second Proculeius?

All   Dolabella!

Caesar   Let him alone, for I remember now
        How he's employed. He shall in time be ready.
        Go with me to my tent, where you shall see
        How hardly[32] I was drawn into this war,
75   How calm and gentle I proceeded still
        In all my writings. Go with me, and see
        What I can show in this.

EXEUNT

30 being alive
31 something eternal / never forgotten in our victory parade
32 uneasily, painfully

SCENE 2

Alexandria, a room in the monument

ENTER CLEOPATRA, CHARMIAN, AND IRAS

Cleopatra My desolation[1] does begin to make
A better life. 'Tis paltry[2] to be Caesar.
Not being Fortune, he's but Fortune's knave,
A minister of her will. And it is great
To do that thing that ends all other deeds,   5
Which shackles[3] accidents and bolts up change,
Which sleeps, and never palates more[4] the dung,
The[5] beggar's nurse and Caesar's.

ENTER, AT THE GATES OF THE MONUMENT,
PROCULEIUS, GALLUS, AND SOLDIERS

Proculeius Caesar sends greeting to the Queen of Egypt,
And bids thee study on what fair demands[6]   10
Thou mean'st to have him grant thee.
Cleopatra   What's thy name?
Proculeius My name is Proculeius.
Cleopatra   Antony
Did tell me of you, bade me trust you, but
I do not greatly care to be deceived,
That[7] have no use for trusting. If your master   15

1 (1) loneliness, being forsaken, (2) devastation, ruined state
2 useless, insignificant
3 chains up
4 palates more = tastes again/any more
5 which is
6 fair demands = reasonable requests
7 I who

Would have a queen his beggar, you must tell him

That majesty, to keep decorum, must

No less beg than a kingdom. If he please

To give me conquered Egypt for my son,

20 He gives me so much of mine own, as[8] I

Will kneel to him with thanks.

Proculeius   Be of good cheer.

You're fall'n into a princely hand, fear nothing,

Make your full reference[9] freely to my lord,

Who is so full of grace that it flows over

25 On all that need. Let me report to him

Your sweet[10] dependency, and you shall find

A conqueror that will pray in aid for kindness,

Where he for grace is kneeled to.

Cleopatra   Pray you, tell him

I am his fortune's vassal, and I send him

30 The greatness he has got. I hourly learn

A doctrine of obedience, and would gladly

Look him i' the face.[11]

Proculeius   This I'll report, dear lady.

Have comfort, for I know your plight is pitied

Of him[12] that caused it.

ENTER GALLUS AND SOLDIERS, FROM BEHIND CLEOPATRA

35 *Gallus*   You see how easily she may be surprised.

(*to Proculeius*) Guard her till Caesar come.

8 so that
9 submissions, requests
10 pleasant, agreeable
11 i.e., meet him
12 Caesar

EXIT GALLUS

Iras	Royal Queen!
Charmian	O Cleopatra, thou art taken, Queen.
Cleopatra	(*drawing a dagger*) Quick, quick, good hands.
Proculeius	Hold,

    worthy lady, hold.

HE SEIZES AND DISARMS HER

    Do not yourself such wrong, who are in this
    Relieved,[13] but not betrayed.

Cleopatra   What, of death too,   40
    That rids our dogs of languish?[14]

Proculeius   Cleopatra,
    Do not abuse my master's bounty by
    The undoing of yourself. Let the world see
    His nobleness well acted, which your death
    Will never let come forth.

Cleopatra   Where art thou, death?   45
    Come hither, come! Come, come, and take a queen
    Worth many babes and beggars!

Proculeius   O temperance, lady!

Cleopatra Sir, I will eat no meat.[15] I'll not drink, sir.
    If idle talk will once[16] be necessary,
    I'll not sleep neither. This mortal house[17] I'll ruin,   50
    Do Caesar what he can. Know sir, that I

13 rescued, freed
14 feebleness, bad health
15 food
16 at any time, ever
17 her body

Will not wait pinioned[18] at your master's court,
Nor once be chastised with the sober eye
Of dull Octavia. Shall they hoist me up
55 And show me to the shouting varletry[19]
Of censuring Rome? Rather a ditch in Egypt
Be gentle grave unto me, rather on Nilus' mud
Lay me stark naked, and let the water-flies
Blow[20] me into abhorring![21] Rather make
60 My country's high pyramids my gibbet,[22]
And hang me up in chains!

Proculeius   You do extend
These thoughts of horror further than you shall
Find cause in Caesar.

ENTER DOLABELLA

Dolabella   Proculeius,
What thou hast done thy master Caesar knows,
65 And he hath sent for thee. For[23] the Queen,
I'll take her to my guard.[24]

Proculeius   So Dolabella,
It shall content me best. Be gentle to her.
(to Cleopatra) To Caesar I will speak what you shall please,
If you'll employ me to him.

Cleopatra   Say, I would[25] die.

18 with wings clipped, shackled
19 menial crowds
20 swell/puff up my corpse
21 (noun) an object of disgust/abhorrence
22 post on which executed bodies were hung for exhibition
23 as for
24 to my guard = into my custody
25 wish to

EXEUNT PROCULEIUS AND SOLDIERS

Dolabella Most noble Empress, you have heard of me? 70

Cleopatra I cannot tell.

Dolabella   Assuredly you know me.

Cleopatra No matter sir, what I have heard or known.
    You laugh when boys or women tell their dreams,
    Is't not your trick?[26]

Dolabella   I understand not, madam.

Cleopatra I dreamed there was an Emperor Antony. 75
    O such another sleep, that I might see
    But such another man!

Dolabella   If it might please ye –

Cleopatra His face was as the heavens, and therein stuck
    A sun and moon, which kept their course, and lighted
    The little O,[27] th' earth.

Dolabella   Most sovereign creature[28] – 80

Cleopatra His legs bestrid[29] the ocean, his reared[30] arm
    Crested the world. His voice was propertied[31]
    As all the tunèd spheres,[32] and that to friends.
    But when he meant to quail and shake the orb,
    He was as rattling thunder. For his bounty, 85
    There was no winter in't, an autumn[33] 'twas

26 stratagem, ruse
27 circle, sphere ("globe")
28 being
29 bestrode (i.e., one leg on each side)
30 raised, lifted
31 had all the qualities / characteristics of
32 i.e., the spheres were supposed to emit a magical music too exalted for
    human ears to hear
33 Folio: Antony; most editors emend

That grew the more by reaping. His delights
Were dolphin-like,[34] they showed his back above
The element they lived in. In his livery[35]
90   Walked crowns and crownets. Realms and islands were
As plates[36] dropped from his pocket.

Dolabella   Cleopatra —

Cleopatra Think you there was, or might be, such a man
As this I dreamed of?

Dolabella   Gentle madam, no.

Cleopatra You lie, up[37] to the hearing of the gods.
95   But if there be, or ever were one such,
It's past the size[38] of dreaming. Nature wants[39] stuff
To vie[40] strange forms with fancy, yet t' imagine
An Antony were nature's piece[41] 'gainst fancy,
Condemning shadows[42] quite.

Dolabella   Hear me, good madam.
100   Your loss is as[43] yourself, great, and you bear it
As answering[44] to the weight. Would I might never
O'ertake pursued success,[45] but I do feel,

34 leaping like dolphins
35 servant uniforms
36 coins
37 directly/straight up
38 standard
39 lacks, is deficient in
40 compete
41 creation
42 condemning shadows = discrediting imaginary things
43 like
44 responding to
45 o'ertake pursued success = catch someone successful who is being chased/
   pursued

By the rebound[46] of yours, a grief that smites
My very heart at root.

Cleopatra   I thank you, sir,
Know you what Caesar means to do with me?   105
Dolabella I am loath to tell you what I would you knew.
Cleopatra Nay, pray you sir –
Dolabella   Though he be honorable –
Cleopatra He'll lead me, then, in triumph?
Dolabella Madam he will, I know't.

FLOURISH

ENTER CAESAR, GALLUS, PROCULEIUS, MAECENAS,
SELEUCUS, AND OTHERS

All   Make way there! Caesar!
Caesar   Which is the Queen of
Egypt?   110
Dolabella It is the Emperor, madam.

CLEOPATRA KNEELS

Caesar   Arise, you shall[47] not kneel.
I pray you rise, rise Egypt.
Cleopatra   (standing) Sir, the gods
Will have it thus, my master and my lord
I must obey.
Caesar   Take to you no hard thoughts.   115
The record of what injuries you did us,
Though written in our flesh, we shall remember

46 extent ("violent blow")
47 must

As things but done by chance.

Cleopatra   Sole sir o' the world,
I cannot project⁴⁸ mine own cause so well

120   To make it clear, but do confess I have
Been laden with like frailties which before
Have often shamed our sex.

Caesar   Cleopatra, know,
We will extenuate⁴⁹ rather than enforce.
If you apply yourself to our intents,

125   Which towards you are most gentle, you shall find
A benefit in this change. But if you seek
To lay on me a cruelty, by taking
Antony's course, you shall bereave⁵⁰ yourself
Of my good purposes, and put your children

130   To that destruction which I'll guard them from,
If thereon you rely. I'll take my leave.

Cleopatra And may, through all the world. 'Tis yours, and we,
Your scutcheons⁵¹ and your signs of conquest, shall
Hang in what place you please. (*hands him document*) Here, my
good lord.

135 Caesar   You shall advise me in all for⁵² Cleopatra.

Cleopatra This is the brief⁵³ of money, plate, and jewels,
I am possessed of, 'tis exactly valued,
Not petty things admitted. Where's Seleucus?

Seleucus   Here, madam.

---

48 set forth, exhibit
49 diminish, reduce, lessen, weaken
50 strip, rob
51 shields and shield-shaped ornaments, representing Caesar's coat of arms
52 all for = everything having to do with
53 summary, list, catalogue

Cleopatra This is my treasurer, let him speak, my lord,   140
   Upon his peril, that I have reserved[54]
   To myself nothing. Speak the truth, Seleucus.
Seleucus Madam,
   I had rather seel my lips, than, to my peril,
   Speak that which is not.
Cleopatra   What have I kept back?   145
Seleucus Enough to purchase what you have made known.
Caesar Nay blush not, Cleopatra, I approve
   Your wisdom in the deed.[55]
Cleopatra   See, Caesar! O behold,
   How pomp is followed![56] Mine will now be yours,
   And should we shift estates,[57] yours would be mine.   150
   The ingratitude of this Seleucus does
   Even[58] make me wild. O slave, of no more trust
   Than love that's hired? What, goest thou back?[59] Thou shalt
   Go back,[60] I warrant thee. But I'll catch[61] thine eyes
   Though they had wings. Slave, soulless villain, dog!   155
   O rarely base!
Caesar   Good queen, let us entreat[62] you.
Cleopatra O Caesar, what a wounding shame is this,
   That thou, vouchsafing here to visit me,
   Doing the honor of thy lordliness

54 kept back, set part
55 in the deed = in so doing
56 served, waited on
57 change conditions
58 precisely, fully
59 goes thou back = are you retreating from me
60 go back = lose ground
61 attack ("scratch/claw out")
62 implore, beseech

160 To one so meek, that mine own servant should
Parcel[63] the sum of my disgraces by
Addition of his envy! Say, good Caesar,
That I some lady trifles have reserved,
Immoment[64] toys, things of such dignity
165 As we greet modern[65] friends withal, and say,
Some nobler token I have kept apart
For Livia and Octavia, to induce[66]
Their mediation,[67] must I be unfolded
With[68] one that I have bred? The gods! It smites me
170 Beneath[69] the fall I have. (*to Seleucus*) Prithee go hence,
Or I shall show the cinders[70] of my spirits
Through the ashes of my chance. Wert thou a man,
Thou wouldst have[71] mercy on me.

Caesar   Forbear, Seleucus.

EXIT SELEUCUS

Cleopatra Be it known, that we the greatest[72] are misthought[73]
175 For things that others do. And when we fall,
We answer others' merits[74] in our name,

63 divide up and distribute
64 trifling, insignificant
65 ordinary, commonplace
66 bring in
67 intercession ("help")
68 unfolded with = exposed by
69 lower than
70 glowing coals, not flaming or burned out
71 have had
72 highest ranking
73 mistakenly thought ("misjudged")
74 demerits

Are[75] therefore to be pitied.

Caesar   Cleopatra,
Not what you have reserved, nor what acknowledged,
Put we i' the roll[76] of conquest. Still[77] be't yours,
Bestow it at your pleasure, and believe   180
Caesar's no merchant, to make prize[78] with you
Of things that merchants sold. Therefore be cheered,
Make not your thoughts your prisons. No dear Queen,
For we intend so to dispose[79] you as
Yourself shall give us counsel. Feed, and sleep.   185
Our care and pity is so much upon you,
That we remain your friend, and so adieu.

Cleopatra My master, and my lord.

Caesar   Not so. Adieu.

FLOURISH

EXEUNT CAESAR AND HIS FOLLOWERS

Cleopatra He words me, girls, he words me, that I should not
Be noble to myself. But hark thee, Charmian.   190

CLEOPATRA WHISPERS TO CHARMIAN

Iras   Finish[80] good lady, the bright day is done,
And we are[81] for the dark.

Cleopatra   Hie thee again,

75 and are
76 official record/listing
77 let it still
78 a match/contest
79 deal with, place, direct, control
80 cease, have done
81 are headed

I have spoke already, and it is provided,
Go put it to the haste.[82]

Charmian   Madam, I will.

ENTER DOLABELLA

Dolabella Where is the Queen?

Charmian   Behold, sir.

EXIT CHARMIAN

195 *Cleopatra*   Dolabella.

Dolabella Madam, as thereto sworn by your command,
     Which my love makes religion[83] to obey,
     I tell you this. Caesar through Syria
     Intends his journey, and within three days
200   You with your children will he send before.
     Make your best use of this. I have performed
     Your pleasure, and my promise.

Cleopatra   Dolabella,
     I shall remain your debtor.

Dolabella   I[84] your servant.
     Adieu good Queen, I must attend on Caesar.

Cleopatra Farewell, and thanks.

EXIT DOLABELLA

205   Now Iras, what think'st thou?
     Thou[85] an Egyptian puppet shalt be shown

82 i.e., hurry it up
83 obligatory
84 I will remain
85 you like

In Rome, as well as I. Mechanic slaves[86]
With greasy aprons, rules,[87] and hammers, shall
Uplift us to the view.[88] In their thick breaths,
Rank of gross[89] diet, shall we be enclouded,   210
And forced to drink[90] their vapor.[91]

Iras   The gods forbid!

Cleopatra Nay, 'tis most certain Iras. Saucy lictors[92]
Will catch at us like strumpets, and scald[93] rhymers
Ballad us out o' tune. The quick comedians
Extemporally will stage us, and present   215
Our Alexandrian revels. Antony
Shall be brought drunken forth, and I shall see
Some squeaking Cleopatra boy[94] my greatness
I' the posture of a whore.

Iras   O the good gods!

Cleopatra Nay, that's certain.   220

Iras   I'll never see 't! For I am sure mine nails
Are stronger than mine eyes.

Cleopatra   Why, that's the way
To fool their preparation, and to conquer
Their most absurd intents.

ENTER CHARMIAN

86 workmen
87 measuring sticks
88 uplift us to the view = raise us up for general inspection (on platforms)
89 rank of gross = rancid from coarse / inferior
90 suck in, inhale
91 breath, exhalation
92 bailiffs
93 scabby, contemptible, paltry
94 (verb) represent, act

Now Charmian,
225 Show me, my women, like a queen. Go fetch
My best attires. I am again for[95] Cydnus,
To meet Mark Antony. Sirrah[96] Iras, go
(Now, noble Charmian, we'll dispatch indeed)
And when thou hast done this chore, I'll give thee leave
230 To play till doomsday. Bring our crown and all.

EXIT IRAS

(*noise within*) Wherefore's this noise?

ENTER A GUARDSMAN

Guard   Here is a rural fellow
That will not be denied your Highness' presence.
He brings you figs.
Cleopatra Let him come in.

EXIT GUARDSMAN

What[97] poor an instrument
235 May do a noble deed. He brings me liberty.
My resolution's placed,[98] and I have nothing
Of woman in me. Now from head to foot
I am marble-constant. Now the fleeting moon
No planet is of mine.

ENTER GUARDSMAN, AND PEASANT WITH A BASKET

95 again for = once again headed for
96 (the word is applicable to both sexes)
97 how
98 set, fixed

Guard	This is the man.
Cleopatra	Avoid,[99] and leave him.

    240

EXIT GUARDSMAN

Hast thou the pretty worm[100] of Nilus there,
That kills and pains not?

Rustic   Truly I have him. But I would not be the party that
should desire you to touch him, for his biting is immortal.
Those that do die of it do seldom or never recover.   245

Cleopatra Rememberest thou any that have died on't?[101]

Rustic   Very many, men and women too. I heard of one of
them no longer than yesterday, a very honest woman, but
something given to lie, as a woman should not do but[102] in
the way of honesty, how she died of the biting of it, what   250
pain she felt. Truly, she makes a very good report o' the
worm. But he that will believe all that they say, shall never
be saved by half that they do. But this is most fallible, the
worm's an odd[103] worm.

Cleopatra Get thee hence, farewell.   255

Rustic   I wish you all joy of the worm.

HE SETS DOWN HIS BASKET

Cleopatra Farewell.

Rustic   You must think this, look you, that the worm will do
his kind.[104]

---

 99 withdraw
100 pretty worm = excellent snake (an asp)
101 of/from it
102 except
103 unique
104 do his kind = do what he as a snake is supposed to do

260 *Cleopatra* Ay, ay, farewell.

    Rustic Look you, the worm is not to be trusted but in the keeping of wise people. For indeed, there is no goodness in the worm.

    Cleopatra Take thou no care, it shall be heeded.

265 *Rustic* Very good. Give it nothing, I pray you, for it is not worth the feeding.

    Cleopatra Will it eat me?

    Rustic You must not think I am so simple but I know the devil himself will not eat a woman. I know that a woman is a

270 dish for the gods, if the devil dress[105] her not. But truly, these same whoreson[106] devils do the gods great harm in their women, for in every ten that they make, the devils mar five.

    Cleopatra Well, get thee gone, farewell.

    Rustic Yes forsooth. I wish you joy o' the worm.

EXIT RUSTIC

ENTER CHARMIAN AND IRAS WITH A ROBE,
A CROWN, AND JEWELS

275 *Cleopatra* Give me my robe, put on my crown, I have
Immortal longings in me. Now no more
The juice of Egypt's grape shall moist this lip.
Yare, yare, good Iras, quick. Methinks I hear
Antony call. I see him rouse himself

280 To praise my noble act. I hear him mock
The luck of Caesar, which the gods give men
To excuse their after[107] wrath. Husband, I come.

105 prepares, manages
106 wretched ("damned")
107 subsequent

Now to that name my[108] courage prove my title.
I am fire, and air, my other elements
I give to baser life.[109] So, have you done?   285
Come then, and take the last warmth of my lips.
Farewell kind Charmian, Iras, long farewell.

CLEOPATRA KISSES THEM, IRAS FALLS AND DIES[110]

Have I the aspic[111] in my lips? Dost fall?
If thou and nature can so gently part,
The stroke of death is as a lover's pinch,   290
Which hurts, and is desired. Dost thou lie still?
If thus thou vanishest, thou tell'st the world
It is not worth leave-taking.[112]

Charmian Dissolve, thick cloud, and rain, that I may say
    The gods themselves do weep!

Cleopatra   This[113] proves me base.   295
If she[114] first meet the curlèd Antony,
He'll make demand of her, and spend that kiss
Which is my heaven to have. (to the asp) Come, thou mortal
    wretch,
With thy sharp teeth this knot intrinsicate[115]
Of life at once untie. (sets it to her breast) Poor venomous fool, 300
Be angry, and dispatch. O couldst thou speak,

---

108 may my
109 (earth and water = baser elements than fire and air)
110 (?) of self-inflicted causes?
111 poison of the asp
112 i.e., bothering to say farewells
113 this thought
114 Iras
115 (adjective) tangled

That I might hear thee call great Caesar ass
Unpolicied![116]
Charmian   O eastern star![117]
Cleopatra   Peace, peace.
Dost thou not see my baby at my breast,
That sucks the nurse asleep?
305 Charmian   O break![118] O break!
Cleopatra   As sweet as balm, as soft as air, as gentle –
O Antony! – (*to another asp, applying it to her arm*) Nay, I will
take thee too.
What[119] should I stay –

Cleopatra dies

Charmian   In this vile world?[120] So fare thee well.
310   Now boast thee death, in thy possession lies
A lass unparalleled. (*closing Cleopatra's eyes*) Downy windows
close,
And golden Phoebus never be beheld
Of[121] eyes again so royal! Your crown's awry,
I'll mend it, and then play –

ENTER GUARDSMEN, RUSTLING[122] IN

Guard 1   Where's the Queen?
315 Charmian   Speak softly, wake her not.

---

116 ass unpolicied = an artless/awkward/imprudent diplomat
117 (usually said of Venus, but here of Cleopatra)
118 may I burst/shatter/dissolve
119 why
120 i.e., finishing Cleopatra's incomplete question
121 by
122 rushing

Guard 1   Caesar hath sent –

Charmian   Too slow a messenger.

    (*she applies an asp*) O come apace, dispatch, I partly[123] feel

    thee.

Guard 1   Approach, ho, all's not well. Caesar's beguiled.

Guard 2   There's Dolabella sent from Caesar. Call him.

Guard 1   What work is here, Charmian? Is this well done?   320

Charmian It is well done, and fitting for a princess

    Descended of so many royal kings.

    Ah soldier –

CHARMIAN DIES

ENTER DOLABELLA

Dolabella   How goes it here?

Guard 2   All dead.

Dolabella   Caesar, thy thoughts

    Touch their effects in this. Thyself art coming   325

    To see performed[124] the dreaded act which thou

    So sought'st to hinder.

ENTER CAESAR AND HIS FOLLOWERS MARCHING

Followers   Within a way there, a way for Caesar!

Dolabella   O sir, you are too sure an augurer.

    That[125] you did fear is done.

Caesar   Bravest at the last,   330

    She leveled[126] at our purposes, and being royal,

---

123 to some degree already
124 accomplished, done
125 that which
126 guessed

Took her own way. The manner of their deaths?
I do not see them bleed.

Dolabella   Who was last with them?

Guard 1   A simple countryman, that brought her figs.
This was his basket.

Caesar   Poisoned, then.

335 *Guard 1*   O Caesar,
This Charmian lived[127] but now, she stood and spake.
I found her trimming up the diadem
On her dead mistress. Tremblingly she stood
And on the sudden dropped.

Caesar   O noble weakness![128]

340 If they had swallowed poison, 'twould appear
By external swelling. But she looks like sleep,[129]
As she would catch another Antony
In her strong toil[130] of grace.

Dolabella   Here on her breast,
There is a vent[131] of blood and something blown,[132]

345 The like is on her arm.

Guard 1   This is an aspic's trail, and these fig leaves
Have slime upon them, such as the aspic leaves
Upon the caves of Nile.

Caesar   Most probable
That so she died. For her physician tells me

350 She hath pursued conclusions infinite

127 was alive
128 i.e., they were women, and weak, but exceedingly noble
129 like sleep = as if she is asleep
130 net (used in hunting)
131 discharge
132 hinted (i.e., the trail of an asp)

Of easy ways to die. Take up her bed,
And bear her women from the monument,
She shall be buried by her Antony.
No grave upon the earth shall clip[133] in it
A pair so famous. High events as these   355
Strike those that make them. And their story is
No less[134] in pity than his glory[135] which
Brought[136] them to be lamented. Our army shall
In solemn show attend this funeral,
And then to Rome. Come Dolabella, see[137]   360
High order[138] in this great solemnity.[139]

EXEUNT

133 enclose
134 no less = not lesser
135 Caesar's own
136 caused
137 make sure that there is
138 rank
139 i.e., the forthcoming funeral

Freud taught us that the therapy-of-therapies is not to invest too much libido in any single object whosoever. Antony at last refuses this wisdom and in consequence suffers what must be called an erotic tragedy, but then Cleopatra, who has spent her life exemplifying the same wisdom, suffers an erotic tragedy also, on Antony's account, one act of the drama more belatedly than he does. *The Tragedy of Antony and Cleopatra* is unique among Shakespeare's plays in that the tragedy's doubleness, equal in both man and woman as it was with Romeo and Juliet, takes place between equally titanic personages. Each truly is all but everything in himself and herself, and *knows* it, and neither fears that he or she is really nothing in himself or herself, or nothing without the other. Both consciously play many parts, and yet also *are* those other parts. Both are adept at playing themselves, yet also at being themselves. Like Falstaff and Hamlet, they are supreme personalities, major wits, grand counter-Machiavels (though overmatched by Octavian, greatest of Machiavels), and supreme consciousnesses. They fall in love with one another, resist and betray the love repeatedly, but finally yield to it and are destroyed by it, in order fully to fulfill their allied natures. More even than the death of Hamlet, we react to their suicides as a human triumph and as a release for ourselves. But why? And how?

The crucial originality here is to have represented two great personalities, the Herculean hero proper and a woman of infinite guile and resource, in their overwhelming decline and mingled ruin. A destruction through authentic and mutual love becomes an aesthetic redemption precisely because love's shadow is ruin. We have no representations of this kind before Shakespeare, since a Euripidean vision of erotic ruin, as in the *Medea,* permits no aesthetic redemption, while Virgil's Dido, like Medea, is a solitary sufferer. Antony and Cleopatra repeatedly betray one another, and betray themselves, yet these betrayals are forgiven by them and by us, since they become phases of apotheosis that release the sparks of grandeur even as the lamps are shattered.

From act 4, scene 14, through to the end of the play, we hear something wonderfully original even for Shakespeare, a great dying fall, the release of a new music. It begins with the dialogue between Antony and his marvelously named, devoted follower, Eros:

Antony Eros, thou yet behold'st me?
Eros   Ay, noble lord.
Antony Sometime we see a cloud that's dragonish,
    A vapor sometime like a bear or lion,
    A towered citadel, a pendent rock,
    A forkèd mountain, or blue promontory
    With trees upon't, that nod unto the world,
    And mock our eyes with air. Thou hast seen these signs,
    They are black vesper's pageants.
Eros   Ay my lord.

Antony That which is now a horse, even with a thought
     The rack dislimns, and makes it indistinct,
     As water is in water.
Eros   It does, my lord.
Antony My good knave Eros, now thy captain is
     Even such a body. Here I am Antony,
     Yet cannot hold this visible shape, my knave.
     I made these wars for Egypt, and the Queen –
     Whose heart I thought I had, for she had mine,
     Which whilst it was mine had annexed unto't
     A million more, now lost – she, Eros, has
     Packed cards with Caesar, and false-played my glory
     Unto an enemy's triumph.
     Nay, weep not gentle Eros, there is left us
     Ourselves to end ourselves.

                                        (lines 1–22)

There is a deliberate touch of the cloud-watching Hamlet in Antony here, but with Hamlet's parodistic savagery modulated into a gentleness that befits the transmutation of the charismatic hero into a self-transcendent consciousness, almost beyond the consolations of farewell. The grandeur of this transformation is enhanced when Antony receives the false tidings Cleopatra sends of her supposed death, with his name her last utterance: "Unarm Eros, the long day's task is done, / And we must sleep."

The answering chorus to that splendor is Cleopatra's, when he dies in her arms:

     The crown o' the earth doth melt. My lord!
     O withered is the garland of the war,
     The soldier's pole is fall'n. Young boys and girls

Are level now with men. The odds is gone,
And there is nothing left remarkable
Beneath the visiting moon.

(lines 63–68)

Antony touches the Sublime as he prepares to die, but Cleopatra's lament for a lost Sublime is the prelude to a greater sublim-
ity, which is to be wholly her own. She is herself a great actress, so
that the difficulty in playing her, for any actress, in quite extraor-
dinary. And though she certainly loved Antony, it is inevitable
that, like any great actress, she must love herself all but apocalyp-
tically. Antony has a largeness about him surpassing any other
Shakespearean hero except for Hamlet; he is an ultimate version
of the charismatic leader, loved and followed because his palpable
glory can be shared, in some degree, since he is also magnificently
generous. But Shakespeare shrewdly ends him with one whole
act of the play to go, and retrospectively we see that the drama is
as much Cleopatra's as the two parts of *Henry IV* are Falstaff's.

Remarkable as Antony is in himself, he interests us primarily
because he has the splendor that makes him as much a catastrophe
for Cleopatra as she is for him. Cleopatra is in love with his exu-
berance, with the preternatural vitality that impresses even Octavian. But she knows, as we do, that Antony lacks her infinite variety. Their love, in Freudian terms, is not narcissistic but anaclitic;
they are propped upon one another, cosmological beings who are
likely to be bored by anyone else, by any personality neither their
own nor one another's. Antony is Cleopatra's only true match
and yet he is not her equal, which may be the most crucial or
deepest meaning of the play. An imaginative being in that he
moves the imagination of others, he is simply not an imaginer of

her stature. He need not play himself; he is Herculean. Cleopatra ceases to play herself only when she is transmuted by his death and its aftermath, and we cannot be sure, even then, that she is not both performing and simultaneously becoming that more transcendent self. Strangely like the dying Hamlet in this single respect, she suggests, at the end, that she stands upon a new threshold of being: "I am fire and air; my other elements / I give to baser life."

Is she no longer the earth of Egypt, or the water of the Nile? We have not exactly thought of her as a devoted mother, despite her children by Julius Caesar and by Antony, but in her dying dialogue with Charmian she transmutes the asps, first into her baby, and then apparently into an Antony she might have brought to birth, as in some sense indeed she did:

Charmian   O eastern star!
Cleopatra   Peace, peace.
   Dost thou not see my baby at my breast,
   That sucks the nurse asleep?
Charmian   O break! O break!
Cleopatra   As sweet as balm, as soft as air, as gentle –
   O Antony! – (*to another asp, applying it to her arm*) Nay, I will
   take thee too.
   What should I stay –

CLEOPATRA DIES

(lines 303–8)

As Lear dies, Kent cries out "Break, heart, I prithee break!" even as Charmian does here, not wishing upon the rack of this tough world to stretch Cleopatra out longer. When Antony's men find him wounded to death, they lament that "the star is fall'n," and that "time is at his period." Charmian's "O eastern star!" associates one dying lover with the other, even as her echo of Kent suggests that the dying Empress of the East is in something like the innocence of Lear's madness. Cleopatra is sucked to sleep as a mother is by a child, or a woman by a lover, and dies in such peace that Octavian, of all men, is moved to the ultimate tribute:

> she looks like sleep,
> As she would catch another Antony
> In her strong toil of grace.
>
> (lines 341–43)

Bewildering us by her final manifestation of her infinite variety, Cleopatra dies into a beyond, a Sublime where actress never trod.

FURTHER READING

This is not a bibliography but a selective set of starting places.

Texts

Shakespeare, William. *The First Folio of Shakespeare,* 2d ed. Edited by Charlton Hinman. Introduction by Peter W. M. Blayney. New York: W. W. Norton, 1996.

Language

Houston, John Porter. *The Rhetoric of Poetry in the Renaissance and Seventeenth Century.* Baton Rouge: Louisiana State University Press, 1983.

————. *Shakespearean Sentences: A Study in Style and Syntax.* Baton Rouge: Louisiana State University Press, 1988.

Kermode, Frank. *Shakespeare's Language.* New York: Farrar, Straus and Giroux, 2000.

Kökeritz, Helge. *Shakespeare's Pronunciation.* New Haven: Yale University Press, 1953.

Lanham, Richard A. *The Motives of Eloquence: Literary Rhetoric in the Renaissance.* New Haven and London: Yale University Press, 1976.

Marcus, Leah S. *Unediting the Renaissance: Shakespeare, Marlowe, Milton.* London: Routledge, 1996.

The Oxford English Dictionary: Second Edition on CD-ROM, version 3.0. New York: Oxford University Press, 2002.

Raffel, Burton. *From Stress to Stress: An Autobiography of English Prosody.* Hamden, Conn.: Archon Books, 1992.

Ronberg, Gert. *A Way with Words: The Language of English Renaissance Literature.* London: Arnold, 1992.

Trousdale, Marion. *Shakespeare and the Rhetoricians.* Chapel Hill: University of North Carolina Press, 1982.

Culture

Bindoff, S.T. *Tudor England.* Baltimore: Penguin, 1950.

Bradbrook, M. C. *Shakespeare: The Poet in His World.* New York: Columbia University Press, 1978.

Brown, Cedric C., ed. *Patronage, Politics, and Literary Tradition in England, 1558–1658.* Detroit, Mich.: Wayne State University Press, 1993.

Bush, Douglas. *Prefaces to Renaissance Literature.* New York: W.W. Norton, 1965.

Buxton, John. *Elizabethan Taste.* London: Harvester, 1963.

Cowan, Alexander. *Urban Europe, 1500–1700.* New York: Oxford University Press, 1998.

Driver, Tom E. *The Sense of History in Greek and Shakespearean Drama.* New York: Columbia University Press, 1960.

Finucci, Valeria, and Regina Schwartz, eds. *Desire in the Renaissance: Psychoanalysis and Literature.* Princeton, N.J.: Princeton University Press, 1994.

Fumerton, Patricia, and Simon Hunt, eds. *Renaissance Culture and the Everyday.* Philadelphia: University of Pennsylvania Press, 1999.

Halliday, F. E. *Shakespeare in His Age.* South Brunswick, N.J.: Yoseloff, 1965.

Harrison, G. B., ed. *The Elizabethan Journals: Being a Record of Those Things Most Talked of During the Years 1591–1597.* Abridged ed. 2 vols. New York: Doubleday Anchor, 1965.

Harrison, William. *The Description of England: The Classic Contemporary [1577] Account of Tudor Social Life.* Edited by Georges Edelen. Washington, D.C.: Folger Shakespeare Library, 1968. Reprint, New York: Dover, 1994.

Jardine, Lisa. "Introduction." In Jardine, *Reading Shakespeare Historically.* London: Routledge, 1996.

———. *Worldly Goods: A New History of the Renaissance.* London: Macmillan, 1996.

Jeanneret, Michel. *A Feast of Words: Banquets and Table Talk in the Renaissance.* Translated by Jeremy Whiteley and Emma Hughes. Chicago: University of Chicago Press, 1991.

Kernan, Alvin. *Shakespeare, the King's Playwright: Theater in the Stuart Court, 1603–1613.* New Haven: Yale University Press, 1995.

Lockyer, Roger. *Tudor and Stuart Britain, 1471–1714.* London: Longmans, 1964.

Norwich, John Julius. *Shakespeare's Kings: The Great Plays and the History of England in the Middle Ages, 1337–1485.* New York: Scribner, 2000.

Rose, Mary Beth, ed. *Renaissance Drama as Cultural History: Essays from Renaissance Drama, 1977–1987.* Evanston, Ill.: Northwestern University Press, 1990.

Schmidgall, Gary. *Shakespeare and the Courtly Aesthetic.* Berkeley: University of California Press, 1981.

Smith, G. Gregory, ed. *Elizabethan Critical Essays.* 2 vols. Oxford: Clarendon Press, 1904.

Tillyard, E. M. W. *The Elizabethan World Picture.* London: Chatto and Windus, 1943. Reprint, Harmondsworth: Penguin, 1963.

Willey, Basil. *The Seventeenth Century Background: Studies in the Thought of the Age in Relation to Poetry and Religion.* New York: Columbia University Press, 1933. Reprint, New York: Doubleday, 1955.

Wilson, F. P. *The Plague in Shakespeare's London.* 2d ed. Oxford: Oxford University Press, 1963.

Wilson, John Dover. *Life in Shakespeare's England: A Book of Elizabethan Prose.* 2d ed. Cambridge: Cambridge University Press, 1913. Reprint, Harmondsworth: Penguin, 1944.

Zimmerman, Susan, and Ronald F. E. Weissman, eds. *Urban Life in the Renaissance.* Newark: University of Delaware Press, 1989.

Dramatic Development

Cohen, Walter. *Drama of a Nation: Public Theater in Renaissance England and Spain.* Ithaca, N.Y.: Cornell University Press, 1985.

Dessen, Alan C. *Shakespeare and the Late Moral Plays.* Lincoln: University of Nebraska Press, 1986.

Fraser, Russell A., and Norman Rabkin, eds. *Drama of the English Renaissance.* 2 vols. Upper Saddle River, N.J.: Prentice Hall, 1976.

Happé, Peter, ed. *Tudor Interludes.* Harmondsworth: Penguin, 1972.

Laroque, François. *Shakespeare's Festive World: Elizabethan Seasonal Entertainment and the Professional Stage.* Translated by Janet Lloyd. Cambridge: Cambridge University Press, 1991.

Norland, Howard B. *Drama in Early Tudor Britain, 1485–1558.* Lincoln: University of Nebraska Press, 1995.

Theater and Stage

Doran, Madeleine. *Endeavors of Art: A Study of Form in Elizabethan Drama.* Milwaukee: University of Wisconsin Press, 1954.

Grene, David. *The Actor in History: Studies in Shakespearean Stage Poetry.* University Park: Pennsylvania State University Press, 1988.

Gurr, Andrew. *Playgoing in Shakespeare's London.* Cambridge: Cambridge University Press, 1987.

———. *The Shakespearian Stage, 1574–1642.* 3d ed. Cambridge: Cambridge University Press, 1992.

Halliday, F. E. *A Shakespeare Companion, 1564–1964.* Rev. ed. Harmondsworth: Penguin, 1964.

Harrison, G. B. *Elizabethan Plays and Players.* Ann Arbor: University of Michigan Press, 1956.

Holmes, Martin. *Shakespeare and His Players.* New York: Scribner, 1972.

Ingram, William. *The Business of Playing: The Beginnings of the Adult Professional Theater in Elizabethan London.* Ithaca, N.Y.: Cornell University Press, 1992.

Lamb, Charles. *The Complete Works and Letters of Charles Lamb.* Edited by Saxe Commins. New York: Modern Library, 1935.

LeWinter, Oswald, ed. *Shakespeare in Europe.* Cleveland, Ohio: Meridian, 1963.

Orgel, Stephen. *The Authentic Shakespeare, and Other Problems of the Early Modern Stage.* New York: Routledge, 2002.

Ornstein, Robert. "The Ethic of the Imagination: Love and Art in *Antony and Cleopatra.*" In Leonard F. Dean, ed., *Shakespeare: Modern Essays in Criticism,* 389–404. Rev. ed. New York: Oxford University Press, 1967.

Salgado, Gamini. *Eyewitnesses of Shakespeare: First Hand Accounts of Performances, 1590–1890.* New York: Barnes and Noble, 1975.

Stern, Tiffany. *Rehearsal from Shakespeare to Sheridan.* Oxford: Clarendon Press, 2000.

Thomson, Peter. *Shakespeare's Professional Career.* Cambridge: Cambridge University Press, 1992.

Webster, Margaret. *Shakespeare without Tears.* New York: Whittlesey House, 1942.

Weimann, Robert. *Shakespeare and the Popular Tradition in the Theater: Studies in the Social Dimension of Dramatic Form and Function.* Edited by Robert Schwartz. Baltimore: Johns Hopkins University Press, 1978.

Wikander, Matthew H. *The Play of Truth and State: Historical Drama from Shakespeare to Brecht.* Baltimore: Johns Hopkins University Press, 1986.

Yachnin, Paul. *Stage-Wrights: Shakespeare, Jonson, Middleton, and the Making of Theatrical Value.* Philadelphia: University of Pennsylvania Press, 1997.

Biography

Halliday, F. E. *The Life of Shakespeare.* Rev. ed. London: Duckworth, 1964.

Honigmann, F. A. J. *Shakespeare: The "Lost Years."* 2d ed. Manchester: Manchester University Press, 1998.

Schoenbaum, Samuel. *Shakespeare's Lives.* New ed. Oxford: Clarendon Press, 1991.

———. *William Shakespeare: A Compact Documentary Life.* Oxford: Oxford University Press, 1977.

General

Bergeron, David M., and Geraldo U. de Sousa. *Shakespeare: A Study and Research Guide.* 3d ed. Lawrence: University of Kansas Press, 1995.

Berryman, John. *Berryman's Shakespeare.* Edited by John Haffenden. Preface by Robert Giroux. New York: Farrar, Straus and Giroux, 1999.

Bradby, Anne, ed. *Shakespearian Criticism, 1919–35*. London: Oxford University Press, 1936.

Colie, Rosalie L. *Shakespeare's Living Art*. Princeton, N.J.: Princeton University Press, 1974.

Dean, Leonard F., ed. *Shakespeare: Modern Essays in Criticism*. Rev. ed. New York: Oxford University Press, 1967.

Goddard, Harold C. *The Meaning of Shakespeare*. 2 vols. Chicago: University of Chicago Press, 1951.

Kaufmann, Ralph J. *Elizabethan Drama: Modern Essays in Criticism*. New York: Oxford University Press, 1961.

McDonald, Russ. *The Bedford Companion to Shakespeare: An Introduction with Documents*. Boston: Bedford, 1996.

Raffel, Burton. *How to Read a Poem*. New York: Meridian, 1984.

Ricks, Christopher, ed. *English Drama to 1710*. Rev. ed. Harmondsworth: Sphere, 1987.

Siegel, Paul N., ed. *His Infinite Variety: Major Shakespearean Criticism Since Johnson*. Philadelphia: Lippincott, 1964.

Sweeting, Elizabeth J. *Early Tudor Criticism: Linguistic and Literary*. Oxford: Blackwell, 1940.

Van Doren, Mark. *Shakespeare*. New York: Holt, 1939.

Weiss, Theodore. *The Breath of Clowns and Kings: Shakespeare's Early Comedies and Histories*. New York: Atheneum, 1971.

Wells, Stanley, ed. *The Cambridge Companion to Shakespeare Studies*. Cambridge, Cambridge University Press, 1986.

FINDING LIST

Repeated unfamiliar words and meanings, alphabetically arranged, with act, scene, and footnote number of first occurrence, in the spelling (form) of that first occurrence

abides	1.3.68	*cheek*	11.42
admired	1.1.70	*chide*	1.1.67
alack	1.2.91	*cloyless*	2.1.9
alarum	3.10.1	*competitor*	1.4.3
amiss	1.4.15	*compose*	2.2.6
apace	1.3.35	*confound*	1.1.61
augurers	4.12.2	*constrained*	3.6.19
beck	3.11.22	*crave*	2.5.34
beguiled	3.7.34	*crownet*	4.12.10
belike	1.2.22	*cunning*	1.2.90
betime	4.4.13	*decorum*	1.2.43
blasted	3.10.4	*detain*	3.6.11
bounty	4.6.9	*discandying*	3.13.87
captain's	1.1.10	*dispatch* (verb)	2.2.85
chance (noun)	2.3.15	*divisions*	2.1.25
chares (noun)	4.15.43	*earing*	1.2.65

Egypt	1.3.28	*Nilus*	1.2.32
else so	1.1.41	*note* (verb)	1.1.71
enforce	1.3.5	*office*	1.1.7
entertainment	3.13.74	*passion*	1.1.68
fair	1.1.69	*patience*	2.5.9
fancy (noun)	2.2.102	*peace* (verb)	3.13.7
fellowship	2.7.7	*petty*	1.5.29
fit	3.3.7	*Phoebus*	1.5.14
flourish (noun)	1.1.17	*place* (noun)	1.2.129
forbear	1.2.72	*Pompeius*	1.2.117
foul	1.2.42	*Pompey*	1.2.119
full	3.13.24	*power*	3.7.26
garboils	1.3.41	*present*	1.2.74
gentle	2.2.1	*prithee*	1.2.24
go to	2.2.60	*purge*	1.3.38
grace	2.2.74	*purpose* (verb)	1.2.109
hark	2.2.7	*question* (noun)	2.2.20
hie (verb)	2.3.4	*quick*	1.2.63
holds	1.3.63	*quite*	2.2.56
honest	1.5.8	*rare*	2.2.106
keep	1.2.43	*resolution*	4.15.29
knave	1.2.42	*retire*	4.4.21
Lethe	2.1.11	*rig* (verb)	2.6.11
list (verb)	4.3.4	*riotous*	1.3.19
marring	3.11.27	*saucy*	3.13.51
mechanic	4.4.20	*seel* (verb)	3.13.56
meetly	1.3.56	*sovereign*	1.3.40
mend	1.2.38	(adjective)	
Misena	2.2.81	*square* (verb)	2.1.23
Neptune	2.7.53	*stomaching*	2.2.5